THE APOSTLES' CREED FOR TODAY

Also Available in the For Today Series:

THE APOSTLES' CREED FOR TODAY

Justo L. González

WJK WESTMINSTER
JOHN KNOX PRESS
LOUISVILLE · KENTUCKY

Book design by Sharon Adams
Cover design by Eric Walljasper, Minneapolis, MN

First edition
Published by Westminster John Knox Press
Louisville, Kentucky

This book is printed on acid-free paper that meets the American National Standards Institute Z39.48 standard. ∞

PRINTED IN THE UNITED STATES OF AMERICA

11 12 13 14 15 16—10 9 8 7 6 5

Library of Congress Cataloging-in-Publication Data is on file at the Library of Congress, Washington, D.C.

ISBN-13: 978-0-664-22933-7
ISBN-10: 0-664-22933-6

The Apostles' Creed

A traditional translation:
I believe in God the Father Almighty, Maker of heaven and earth.

And in Jesus Christ his only Son our Lord; who was conceived by the Holy Ghost, born of the Virgin Mary, suffered under Pontius Pilate, was crucified, dead, and buried; he descended into hell; the third day he rose again from the dead; he ascended into heaven, and sitteth on the right hand of God the Father Almighty; from thence he shall come to judge the quick and the dead.

I believe in the Holy Ghost; the holy catholic church; the communion of saints; the forgiveness of sins; the resurrection of the body; and the life everlasting.

A more modern translation:
I believe in God the Father Almighty, Maker of heaven and earth.

And in Jesus Christ his only Son our Lord; who was conceived by the Holy Spirit, born of the Virgin Mary, suffered under Pontius Pilate, was crucified, dead, and buried; he descended to the dead. On the third day he rose again; he ascended into heaven, is seated at the right hand of the Father, and will come again to judge the living and the dead.

I believe in the Holy Spirit, the holy catholic church, the communion of saints, the forgiveness of sins, the resurrection of the body, and the life everlasting.

Contents

Series Introduction

*T*he For Today series is intended to provide reliable and accessible resources for the study of important biblical texts, theological documents, and Christian practices. The series is written by experts who are committed to making the results of their studies available to those with no particular biblical or theological training. The goal is to provide an engaging means to study texts and practices that are familiar to laity in churches. The authors are all committed to the importance of their topics and to communicating the significance of their understandings to a wide audience. The emphasis is not only on what these subjects have meant in the past but also on their value in the present—"For Today." Our hope is that the books in this series will find eager readers in churches, particularly in the context of education classes. The authors are educators and pastors who wish to engage church laity in the issues raised by their topics. They seek to provide guidance for learning, for nurture, and for growth in Christian experience. To enhance the educational usefulness of these volumes, questions for discussion are included at the end of each chapter. We hope the books in this series will be important resources to enhance Christian faith and life.

The Publisher

Preface

*W*hile I am honored for the opportunity to write this book, it has also been a sad task. It was originally assigned to my friend and colleague Dr. Shirley Guthrie shortly before he was diagnosed with a fatal illness and died. While he had been enthusiastic about this project, he had hardly moved beyond his preface. There he stated the purpose of this book with magisterial clarity and depth that I could never equal:

Sunday after Sunday the minister or worship leader says, "Let us stand and say what we believe, using the words of the Apostles' Creed."

Some members of the congregation find it very meaningful to recite these old familiar words, remembering that fellow Christians of many church traditions have been confessing them for almost two thousand years, and knowing that this very day all over the world, in all the languages of the world, fellow Christians will say the Creed as they gather for worship.

Others will recite the Creed mechanically, without giving much thought to the content and meaning of what they are saying.

Then there are some newer and also older Christians and church members who are not sure that they can honestly affirm what the Creed says. They either repeat the words with a guilty conscience, simply stand there silent, or perhaps edit the Creed to recite some statements and delete others. They have questions and reservations. . . .

Should I say these words when I do not understand what they mean or why they are important, and when I am pretty sure I do not agree with some of them?

Why do we need this or any other creed anyway? Shouldn't we look to God's Word in the Bible rather than to some ancient or modern human words from the church to find out what we are to believe and do?

This ancient creed may have made sense and been helpful a long time ago, but it is pretty irrelevant for people in the modern world. . . .

Isn't it just "official" statements of Christian orthodoxy that divide the church into self-righteous, arrogant, warring parties certain that their understanding of Christian faith and life is right and anyone who disagrees with them is wrong? Isn't it just "orthodox" Christianity, Judaism, and Islam that cause much of the worldwide conflict . . . ?

This book is especially for Christians who struggle with questions like these. Not because they are doubters or heretics who need to be converted to the traditional faith of the church expressed in the Apostles' Creed, but because the church needs them. It needs their disturbing questions that invite all of us to take as seriously as they the decision we are called to make when we stand to say "I believe" . . .

It is thus that Shirley envisioned this project. I have sought to be faithful to his intent but have not attempted to guess what he would have said. I have tried to face the challenges posed by his words in my own way but also in a way that will honor both his memory and the faith we shared.

Introduction

The Origin of the Creed: Fact and Fiction

Where did the Apostles' Creed come from? According to a legend dating to the fourth century, as the twelve apostles prepared to leave Jerusalem and undertake their mission to various parts of the world, they conferred about the contents of their preaching, each contributing what he deemed best, and thus was the Apostles' Creed formed.[1]

As the legend passed from one generation to another, it was further embellished. By the sixth century, in a sermon wrongly attributed to Augustine, we are told that this incident happened on the very day of Pentecost. In order to make the apostles capable of carrying the message of Jesus throughout the world, the Spirit gave them the gift of speaking in all tongues and also inspired the various clauses of the Creed to them—which obviously gave the Creed an authority at least on a par with Scripture. According to this version of the story, each of the twelve, led by the Spirit, proposed a particular clause, as follows:

> **Peter:** "I believe in God the Father Almighty, Maker of heaven and earth."
>
> **Andrew:** "And in Jesus Christ his only Son our Lord."
>
> **James:** "Who was conceived by the Holy Spirit, born of the Virgin Mary."
>
> **John:** "Was crucified, dead, and buried."

Thomas:	"He descended to the dead. On the third day he rose again."
James:	"He ascended into heaven, is seated at the right hand of the Father."
Philip:	"And will come again to judge the living and the dead."
Bartholomew:	"I believe in the Holy Spirit."
Matthew:	"The holy catholic church, the communion of saints."
Simon:	"The forgiveness of sins."
Thaddaeus:	"The resurrection of the flesh."
Matthias:	"Life everlasting."[2]

This legend held sway throughout the Middle Ages, although there were some who confessed their difficulty in actually dividing the Creed into twelve statements, a division which is clearly arbitrary. The only questioning came from the Eastern—Greek and Russian—churches. These had never employed the Apostles' Creed, whose use was limited to the Latin-speaking West. As relations between the Eastern and Western churches became increasingly tense, these Eastern churches tended to think that the so-called Apostles' Creed was a fairly recent invention of the Western churches in order to claim that they had an older and more authoritative statement of faith than the one Eastern churches had—namely, the Nicene Creed, clearly dating from the fourth century. In this they were partly right and partly mistaken, for the Apostles' Creed, although clearly not the work of the apostles, is indeed older than the Nicene.

It was not until the fifteenth century, just before the Protestant Reformation, that Western scholars began questioning the legends about the origins of the Creed. Still, it took two more centuries for scholars to come to the general conclusions now held by most historians—even though there are still disagreements over some details.

On the basis of these studies, we now know that the origins of the Apostles' Creed can be traced back only as far as the middle of the second century, where a formula very similar to the Creed itself was used in Rome.[3] Scholars call that formula, very similar to our Apostles' Creed, and certainly an earlier form of it, "R"—for Rome, its apparent place of origin. The essential outline of R seems to have had widespread acceptance, for second-century Christian writers from as far away as Gaul and North Africa, when seeking to summarize the "rule of faith," employ a very similar wording.[4]

The basic structure of R, and then of the Apostles' Creed—and of other ancient creeds—comes from their connection with baptism. Although it is possible—with some imagination and creativity—to divide the Creed into twelve clauses in order to assign one to each apostle, in fact the structure of the Creed has evolved from the ancient baptismal formula "in the name of the Father, and the Son, and the Holy Spirit." Thus, the Creed itself has three main parts, one referring to each of the three persons of the Trinity—although, for reasons that will become clear later, the section referring to the Son is much more detailed than the other two.

Apparently, while R or some form of it was used in Rome and in churches related to it, particularly in Western Europe and North Africa, other churches employed other creedal formulas. While all of these were Trinitarian in structure, their actual content varied according to the emphases in a particular region, and especially according to the challenges a church was facing as its creed evolved.

The earliest form of R seems to have been interrogatory: Do you believe in . . . ? These were the questions asked of a neophyte at the point of baptism, apparently when already in the water and before each of three immersions or pourings of water over the head. Yet it is clear that there must have been a period of teaching before baptism, so that candidates would know what it was that they were affirming. This period is the origin of our present-day Lent, for baptisms usually took place on the night before Easter. At least by the fourth century, the Creed was the high point of preparation for baptism. In the early stages of that preparation, very little was said about Christian doctrine. Candidates for baptism attended the early part of worship services—the "Service of the Word"—and there heard Scripture read and explained. But their actual preparation for baptism consisted mostly in moral teaching, which was particularly necessary in a society where many practices rejected by Christianity were generally accepted. Toward the end of their preparation for baptism, candidates finally had the Creed taught and explained to them. It was almost as if the Creed were too important to trust to any but those who had already proven morally ready for baptism; in many cases the Lord's Prayer was treated with equal reverence. At the point where it was clear who was morally ready for baptism, such persons were declared "competent," and the bishop—the pastor—taught and explained the Creed to them. This was the "giving of the faith" or the "giving of the Creed." Once candidates had learned the Creed and its meaning— usually through several sessions of teaching and explanation—there was the "returning of the faith," in which they recited the Creed back to the bishop, apparently sometimes before the congregation and sometimes just before entering the baptismal waters. Then, at the very point of their baptism, as a further affirmation of faith, they were presented with the Creed once again, although now in its ancient interrogatory form: Do you believe in . . . ? This meant that for the congregation at large, reciting the Creed was a reaffirmation of the faith they had declared at their baptism and thus was part of a renewal of their baptismal vows.

It was only after the empire and society at large became Christian—at least nominally—in the fourth century, and practically all were baptized as infants, that this use of the Creed became less and less prevalent, for it was impossible to teach the Creed to infants. At that point, the Creed became what it is for many of us today: a simple declaration of the faith of the church, with little or no connection to our baptism.

The Purpose of the Creed: Fact and Fiction

The differences among the various creeds—and the evolution of R itself—show that there is another common notion regarding creeds that is not quite true. We tend to think that the purpose of a creed is to summarize all the content of Christian doctrine. But in fact creeds were composed in order to bolster particular points of doctrine that were under attack—which is precisely the reason why there is so much in the Apostles' Creed about Jesus and so little about the Holy

Spirit. This also explains the silence of the Apostles' Creed on matters such as Scripture, the sacraments, and many others.

Thus, the original purpose of most ancient creeds was to affirm faith in the Trinity—Father, Son, and Holy Spirit—and to bolster believers against those views that at the time seemed the greatest threats to Christian faith—views the church saw as contradicting some of the essential points of Christian faith. On the other hand, the Apostles' Creed—or at least R—was composed when Christianity was trying to define its own identity in the midst of a society where all sorts of religions vied for people's allegiance. In this sense, it clearly sought to be "apostolic." Its purpose was to define the identity of Christianity in the midst of the wide variety of religions, superstitions, and syncretistic belief systems circulating in the first centuries of the Christian era. For this reason, the Creed does serve to remind us of some of the central doctrines defining the identity of Christianity: the universal power of God, creation, the incarnation, death and resurrection of Jesus, and the presence and work of the Holy Spirit.

In consequence, while it is true that all creeds are historically conditioned, reflecting the prevailing views when they were composed and emphasizing those points of doctrine that seemed to be most threatened at the time, it is also true that the Apostles' Creed has permanent value for the church. It reminds us of some of the central points of the gospel and invites us to count ourselves among the many throughout the generations who have expressed their faith in its words.

The Universal Use of the Apostles' Creed: Fact and Fiction

For most Protestants and Roman Catholics, "the Creed" is the Apostles' Creed. Since in both Catholic and Protestant churches it is used more commonly than other statements of faith, one often hears that it is the most commonly accepted creed of the ancient church. But this is not quite true. R, and later the Apostles' Creed, were essentially the product of the church in Rome, and therefore the Apostles' Creed is widely used only in those churches that somehow trace their origins to Western, Latin-speaking Christianity. At the same time when R was evolving into our present-day Apostles' Creed, the Eastern, Greek-speaking churches had a number of creeds used in connection with baptism in much the same way as R was used in Rome. When in the year 325 a great council of bishops representing the entire church was gathered at Nicaea, they agreed on a creed to be used henceforth by all churches. With some later additions and variations, this is what we now call the Nicene Creed, accepted by both Eastern and Western churches. Therefore, if one asks a Greek or Russian Orthodox Christian to recite "the Creed," one will not hear the familiar words, "I believe in God the Father Almighty," but rather, "We believe in one God the Father Almighty, maker of heaven and earth and of all things visible and invisible." Later on, in various points in the course of this study, I shall have opportunity to say more about the Nicene Creed and how and why it differs from the Apostles' Creed. For the present, however, suffice it to say that the Nicene Creed, although less familiar among Western Christians, is more widely accepted than the Apostles' Creed.

In the West, the Apostles' Creed tended to eclipse the Nicene, at first primarily because of its simplicity. The Nicene Creed, being a response to the rather sophisticated Arian movement, and seeking to counteract its teachings, is much more difficult to understand and even to memorize. In contrast, the Apostles' Creed focuses on the life of Jesus, following a chronological order that can be learned fairly easily: "born . . . suffered . . . was crucified, dead, and buried . . . descended . . . rose . . . ascended . . . is seated . . . will come." By the middle of the fifth century, some people recited it twice a day as a reminder of their faith and perhaps even as a talisman against evil in general.

Then in the ninth century, when controversy raged because of a word that the Western Church had added to the Nicene Creed—the *filioque*, to which we shall return—the papacy found itself in a difficult position, between the still powerful Byzantine Empire, which insisted on the original wording of the Nicene Creed, and the even more powerful Carolingian Empire, which insisted on the newer version. Partly as a way to avoid taking sides, the ancient Roman Creed now known as the Apostles' Creed was promoted both by the papacy and by others seeking to avoid conflict. At the time of the Reformation, Luther, Calvin, and the Church of England all affirmed the value of the Apostles' Creed as a summary of doctrine to be recited regularly—and sometimes to be used as the outline for catechisms. But all of them continued employing and acknowledging the authority of the Nicene Creed.

Thus, while the East continued reciting the Nicene formula as "the Creed," the West progressively abandoned it in favor of the Apostles' Creed, while still affirming the authority of the Nicene formula. This means that, as far as official ecclesiastical endorsement is concerned, the Nicene Creed has much wider acceptance than the Apostles', while the latter enjoys much wider actual use in most denominations derived from the Western Church—that is, Roman Catholics and Protestants.

Even so, since this book deals primarily with the Apostles' Creed, from this point on I shall refer to it simply as "the Creed," and to the other as "the Nicene Creed."

The Creed as a Personal Statement of Faith: Fact and Fiction

There are many Christians today who are uncomfortable reciting the Apostles' Creed—and rightly so. Indeed, the Creed affirms many things that individual Christians find hard to believe. For this reason, they would rather not have the Creed recited in worship, and when it is recited they either skip those phrases they do not believe, or they utter them with a deep feeling of unease, believing themselves to be hypocrites by mouthing things they do not believe. Still others simply mumble along, so as not to attract attention to themselves.

At this point, it would be helpful to think of the Creed not so much as a personal statement of faith but rather as a statement of what it is that makes the church be the church, and of our allegiance to the essence of the gospel and therefore to the church that proclaims it.

To understand what this means, we may look at the Pledge of Allegiance. People recite it at various times as a sign of patriotism, as an indication that they truly stand for the flag and with "the Republic for which it stands." Yet when you stop to think about it, there are statements in that pledge that many who recite it would personally question—or at least interpret in their own particular way. To declare, for instance, that the nation is "indivisible" is to forget the horrors of the Civil War—or perhaps to remember them so vividly that they must be avoided at all costs. It is also to ignore the many racial, political, social, and economic divisions within the country and to ignore the way many exploit and foster such divisions for personal gain. And many who affirm that this indivisible nation lives "with liberty and justice for all" would question that there is indeed equal justice for all, pointing to the many cases where justice is miscarried, where the innocent suffer, where the guilty go unpunished, where the poor lack basic resources, and so forth.

In spite of all this, we do not take a poll to determine which parts of the Pledge of Allegiance to keep and which to ignore. We do not do this because the pledge is not so much a description of what each citizen as an individual believes as it is a statement of the way the nation sees itself—the way it sees itself, partly in actual fact, and partly as an ideal.

Something similar happens in the case of the Creed. It is not so much *my* statement of faith as it is a statement of the faith of the church through the centuries—a statement that shapes the identity of the church, much as the Pledge of Allegiance shapes the identity of the nation.

There is a story about a young Orthodox priest who told his spiritual adviser that he had difficulties with some of the statements of the Nicene Creed.

"Recite it anyhow," the adviser replied.

The young man came back after a few days, again declaring that he could not in good conscience claim to believe all that the Creed said.

"Recite it anyhow," the older man insisted.

This went on for several weeks, until finally, exasperated and confused, the young priest asked, "Why do you insist I repeat the Creed, when you know there are in it some phrases I don't really believe?"

To which the elderly adviser replied; "Because it is not *your* creed. It is the Creed of the church. When you recite it you are not directly saying what *you* believe. You are declaring what *the church* believes. And you are declaring yourself part of that church, no matter whether you believe every point of doctrine or not."

The same is true for each one of us when it comes to the Apostles' Creed. Were I to write my own creed, I would probably leave out one or two phrases and add some others of my own. I might find it easier to delete the phrase about the virgin birth. And I certainly would want to add something about the social responsibility of believers, about the place of worship in the life of the church, and a number of other items. But when I recite the Apostles' Creed I am declaring myself part of that countless multitude throughout the centuries who have found their identity in the same gospel and the same community of believers of which I am now a part—a multitude that includes martyrs, saints, missionaries, and great theologians, but where in the final analysis all are nothing but redeemed sinners, just as I am.

This may serve as a guideline in our study of the Creed. We must discuss it as openly and as frankly as we can. Where we have difficulties, we must acknowledge them. Hiding them serves no real purpose. At the same time, we are not studying the Creed in order to pick and choose which parts of it we like and which we dislike, but rather in order to understand more about the faith of this people of God whose members we declare ourselves to be—much as a citizen recites the Pledge of Allegiance, both with searching questions about what is being said and with a profound commitment to the people whose identity is expressed in it.

Questions for Discussion

1. In what ways is your appreciation for the Creed enhanced by understanding its historical development?
2. What things are important to you when you affirm your part in the church by reciting the Creed?
3. If you were to construct your own creed, what parts of the Apostles' Creed would you leave out? What other theological statements would you add?

1

I Believe in God the Father

Various Levels of Belief

What do we mean when we say, "I believe"? The phrase itself has several meanings. At its lowest level, it implies uncertainty. Someone asks us, "Did Joe tell Mary that I was coming?" and we reply, "I believe so." In this case what we mean is that we have reason to think that Joe actually told Mary, but we cannot guarantee it. Perhaps Joe was supposed to tell Mary but may have forgotten. Or perhaps Joe told us that he did tell Mary, but we do not quite trust Joe, and we express our distrust by simply saying, "I believe so."

At a slightly higher level, we say "I believe" when expressing an opinion we are willing to support but of which we are not absolutely certain. By saying "I believe," we are signaling that we are willing to discuss the matter and are ready to be convinced that we were wrong. At this level, "I believe" is a synonym for "I think." If I say, for instance, "I believe Isabella pawned her jewels in order to finance Columbus's dream," what I mean is that I think that to be the case but can be persuaded otherwise. In this particular case, if I study the matter further, I will find out that this commonly held notion is not true, and at the end of my inquiry I will say that "I no longer believe" what I used to. On the other hand, if I had said, "I believe that Columbus sailed with three ships," after further inquiry I will no longer say that "I believe," but rather that "I know."

At a still higher level, I may say "I believe" meaning that I am convinced that something is true, even though others might not think so. This may be the result of my own inquiry, or it may be simply a decision I have made for my own personal reasons. At this level some declare, "I believe that God exists," while others, with equal conviction, declare, "I believe that God does not exist," and still others, "I believe that one cannot really know whether God exists or not." For many, this is what is meant when we say, "I believe in God the Father Almighty."

Sometimes when we introduce a sentence by saying "I believe," what we mean is that we are absolutely convinced of something—in some cases even to the point of risking our lives for its sake. This was the case of Charles Findlay, the Cuban doctor who declared, "I believe that yellow fever is transmitted by mosquitoes." He was sufficiently convinced of his belief that he had himself placed in a room with several patients suffering from yellow fever, with screening to keep mosquitoes out of the room. When he came out of this risky test, he was certain that yellow fever is indeed transmitted by mosquitoes. At this level, "belief" is tantamount to "conviction" and is ready to be tested in order to become certainty and to prove its point to others who may not share the same belief.

But there is still another, deeper level at which one may say, "I believe in. . . ." At this level, belief is close to trust. If a child is willing to jump off a ledge into her father's arms, we say that the child is willing because she "believes in" her father, or because she trusts him. At this point, we begin to see the difference between "believing that" and "believing in." What the Creed means when we affirm that "I believe in God" is not merely that we believe that God exists—that we are of the opinion that God exists, or that, after due consideration, we have decided that God exists, or even that we are absolutely convinced that God exists. What the Creed means is that we trust God, that we are willing to stake our lives on God, just as a child jumping off a ledge stakes her life on her father.

Believing *In*

In continuing to explore the various meanings of the phrase "I believe in," we discover that even trust is not enough. When we say we are *in* a house, we mean that our whole being is in it. When we say that we live *in* a particular nation, we are not saying only that we reside there, for it is possible to reside somewhere, but not really live there at all, to be always pining for a different place. We mean also that it is in that nation that we have roots, that—at least for the present—we have settled there, that it is that nation that provides the normal context for our lives.

Thus, when we declare, "I believe in God," we are not saying only that we believe that God exists. Certainly, believing *in* God requires believing also *that* there is a God. But this is not the main thrust of our words. Their main thrust is that we trust God for our lives, and also that it is in this God that we live and believe, that this God is both the foundation and the context of all our belief.

The same is true of the entire Creed. Note that there are three persons in whom we believe: God the Father Almighty, Jesus Christ his Son, and the Holy Spirit. In this sense, it is only *in* God that we believe. We certainly believe that God is "Maker of heaven and earth," and therefore we affirm the doctrine of creation. Likewise, we affirm the resurrection of the dead. Yet strictly speaking, these are things *that* we believe, and not things *in* which we believe.

Reformed theologian Karl Barth has expressed this as follows:

> This "I believe" is consummated in a meeting with One who is not man but God, the Father, Son, and Holy Spirit, and by my believing I see myself completely filled and determined by this object of my faith. And what interests me is not my faith, but He in whom I believe.[1]

God as Father in the Teachings of Jesus

The Creed begins by declaring faith—belief in—"God the Father." What does this mean? For most of us, to speak of God as "Father"— or as "Mother," or as "Father/Mother"—means that God is loving and close to us. This is certainly what Jesus, and a long Jewish tradition before him, meant when he told his disciples about "your Father," when he taught them to pray, "Our Father," and when he referred to God as "my Father." Jesus was speaking mostly to relatively poor fishers and peasants who lived in a social framework where a father was responsible for providing food and shelter, as well as loving care, to his children. His hearers could readily understand when he spoke to them of God as a father watching over his children, or as a father whose child asks for bread or for an egg.

This is also the setting of the parable of the Prodigal Son, in which a father's relationship to his sons is direct, and where this relationship is one of such love that much is forgiven and where the son's return to the household is the occasion for a great feast. In that parable, the son who begrudges his father's enthusiastic and generous reception of his wayward brother does not understand what this loving fatherhood is all about. Yet his father takes the time to explain to him why he is receiving the prodigal with such a feast, apparently hoping that the stubborn son will come to understand what family love is all about.

The Creed in Its Context

This, however, was not the setting in which the Creed took shape. Its original context was a church set at the very heart—the very capital—of the Roman Empire. In traditional Roman society, the figure of a father was not first of all a loving figure but rather a powerful one. The father of the family—the *paterfamilias*—ruled over it as a master, and was often a distant figure. His authority over his children remained until he decided to emancipate them, which he was not obliged to do no matter how old they were. But he was also the *paterfamilias* of the entire household—women, children, grandchildren, slaves, and even freedmen and freedwomen, who still owed him a certain obedience and service.

In a church such as that of Rome in the second century, there would be many who knew no father but their master or *paterfamilias*. Some would be slaves whose natural father had abandoned them in the open—as was quite legal and acceptable in the case of unwanted children—to die of exposure or to be picked up by someone in order to raise them until they could sell them into slavery.[2] Others would be women married off by their father for his own convenience or gain. If the man they married was the *paterfamilias*, they would be directly subject to him. If not, they and their husbands would be subject to whoever held that position in the household.

This is why many of the early Christian writers used the term "God the Father" to refer to God's otherness, to God beyond all human thought, to God as the distant and unknowable source of all things. Roughly at the same time that the Creed was taking shape in Rome, Justin Martyr was writing that God the Father is beyond all human knowledge and does not even relate directly to this mutable world; it is rather God the Son—the Word of God—who relates to the world. It was God the Son who walked in the garden, God the Son who appeared to Moses in the burning bush, and God the Son who led Israel out of Egypt. The Father—like a tyrannical *paterfamilias*—was too highly placed and too distant for such matters.

When Christians in Rome in the second century recited the Creed in its earliest form, probably most of them were not thinking of its first clause as referring primarily to a loving father but to the supreme *paterfamilias*, the ruler of all.

The Ruler of All

This point is reinforced by the very next word in the Creed—the word we now translate as "almighty," whose full import we will explore in the next chapter. In the original Greek, this word is *pantokrator*. This word has a double root, being derived from *pan* and from *krasis*. The first of these is the same prefix we still use in words such as "pan-American," meaning encompassing all the Americas, and "pan-Hellenic," meaning encompassing all Greeks. *Krasis* means "government or rule," and its derivatives are still used in words such as "democracy," government by the people, and "theocracy," goverment by God or by those who claim to be God's representatives. Thus, to say that God is *pantokrator* means first and foremost that God is the ruler of all. It is not, as we tend to think today, a statement about God's power to do any and all things.

In short, to a member of a traditional family in Rome—particularly to one whose relationship with the *paterfamilias* was rather distant, as was probably the case with most Christians in the city—the declaration of belief in "God the Father Almighty" would not immediately bring to mind images of love and care, but rather images of power and authority.

While we now view parenthood—and particularly fatherhood—in a totally different way, it is important for us to understand this, for the

Creed, while certainly affirming faith in a loving God, also takes into account God's mighty power and sovereign authority.

How would early Christians reciting this Creed respond to such a statement? It is impossible for us to know, but we can at least surmise that Christians would respond in a variety of ways. It is possible that some would respond negatively, finding it difficult to relate God to their experience of an earthly and perhaps overbearing *paterfamilias*. Today many women and men who have had abusive or distant fathers prefer not to speak of God as "Father," and even find the idea itself offensive. One may well imagine such a reaction from a son who had been denied his freedom by his father, or from a slave who was treated cruelly by his *paterfamilias*.

But then there is another possible reaction. Some years ago a friend who is a Roman Catholic nun told me that her father had been an abusive alcoholic and that to her as a teenager what was attractive in the Christian message was the offer of a different Father. Her friends and peers had loving fathers who cared for them and who hurried home to be with their children. In contrast, she had a father who did not really care for her, and who often came home late at night, drunk, and shouting abuse at her and all others in the family. She felt deeply deprived until she discovered God as a Father—as a Father who cared for her.

One may surmise that upon reciting the words of the Creed, many believers have felt as did my friend. They had never really had a natural father to care for them. Some may have been left to die by their natural fathers and then picked up by a supposedly foster father whose only purpose was to sell them into slavery. But now they had become Christians and could claim another Father who did care for them— one powerful beyond the most powerful *paterfamilias*. This Father did not rule over a particular household, as did the fathers they experienced in daily life, but over all. This one was the Almighty, the *pantokrator*, the ruler of all!

Subversive Overtones

When seen in this context, the naming of God as Father both affirmed the power and authority of God and limited the power and authority of earthly fathers—in ancient Rome, of the *paterfamilias*. It even had subversive overtones, questioning or at least limiting and relativizing the authority of those whom the existing social order had placed above many confessing this faith. I may be a slave or a wife ordered to be submissive to the head of my household, but I now belong to another household with a very different—and much more powerful—head. No wonder, then, that the Creed was not taught to believers until they had proven their faithfulness and commitment over a long period and were ready to be baptized! At this point, they had to decide whether they would confess this Almighty Father—even though this may prove costly in actual life, perhaps even provoking the wrath of those who had "fatherly" authority over them.[3]

God as Father Today

Time has gone by, and today we live in different social circumstances. We no longer live in a society where fathers have power of life and death over their children—nor even in one where physically abusive parents are legally and socially tolerated. Also, through a process that has been evolving over the last two centuries, we have come to idealize the family and parents' role in it, so that the notion that immediately comes to mind when we hear that God is Father is that God follows Dr. Spock's prescription in dealing with us!

Thus, when we today recite the Apostles' Creed, we interpret its very first words as an affirmation of God's loving closeness to us. This is as it should be, for our God is indeed loving and close to us as a parent is supposed to be, and we do well in affirming and proclaiming this faith and this experience.

Yet there are many today, both men and women, who object to this depiction of God. It seems to give God a masculine character and to neglect the many biblical images in which God is depicted with what society considers feminine, mothering traits. It is too close to the notion that men are somehow more in the image of God than are women. It seems to bolster a patriarchal view of the family, where the father rules the household and the mother and children simply obey and support the father's decisions. From this patriarchal view of the family it is quite easy to move on to tyranny and abuse. For this reason, they prefer to speak of God as "Parent," or as "Mother/Father." These views and feelings deserve respect, both because they point to injustices in society and in the church, and because they often express deeply felt experiences and hurts.

At this point, it may be helpful for all of us to recover some of the subversive overtones of the Creed when it was first composed. By declaring God to be Father, the Creed was undermining fatherhood as it was then understood. Slaves, children, wives, and all others subject to the *paterfamilias* were claiming a Father above this earthly one. However, as the result of a process of centuries, the sharp cutting edge of this faith has been blunted, so that we tend to think that by calling God "Father" we are simply saying that God is "like a father," forgetting that this faith also affirms that we have a Father—or a Mother—high above our earthly father or mother. Thus, when we call God "Father," or "Mother," or even "Father/Mother," we must keep in mind the power that such statements have to subvert our common notions of parenthood—fatherhood and motherhood—and even of family. In this regard, the words of Jesus gain new meaning: "And call no one your father on earth, for you have one Father—the one in heaven" (Matt. 23:9).

One way to approach this matter is to reverse the direction of the analogy. We tend to think that when we call God "Father" or "Mother" what we mean is that God is like a mother or like a father. However, if we reverse the direction of the image, what we are declaring is that mothers and fathers are called to be as loving as God is—and the rest of the Creed, as well as the entire Christian faith, is a statement of God's love for us and for all creation.

This is not to say that there is no place for the authority of earthly parents. There certainly is. But—like God's authority over us—it promotes freedom and development. By declaring that God is our Parent—Father and/or Mother—we are implying that all of us, parents as well as children, are in fact siblings in the great family of God. A Christian may be a father or a mother to a son or daughter, but ultimately they are all brothers and sisters.

Belief *in* God

It is *in* this loving, parenting God, that we believe. This means that it is in this God that all our belief is founded. To say that we believe *in* God is to say that it is in God that all our life exists, including our life of faith. Thus, while the Creed begins with the word *I*, it is not I who is important. The Creed is not ultimately about what I believe: It is rather about the One in whom I believe: "God the Father Almighty."

Questions for Discussion

1. Why is it important to focus on the "object" of our believing (God), rather than in the action of our believing itself?
2. Why is maintaining that God is "ruler of all" as well as "Father" important?
3. In what way is using a parental image for God subversive in our society today?

2

Almighty, Maker of Heaven and Earth

A Later Addition

The early ancestor of our present-day Apostles' Creed—the formula known as "R"—did not include the words "Maker of
heaven and earth." Yet these were added very soon, and from
that point all versions of what eventually became the Apostles'
Creed include them. Why? Probably for two reasons.

The first reason was simply that most other creeds included
a similar phrase. Such is the case, for instance, in the Nicene
Creed, which includes the words "Maker of heaven and earth,
of all that is, seen and unseen." As Western Christians—who
were the only ones using R—had increasing contact with other
believers, and as they alternated this creed with the Nicene, it
was inevitable that a phrase obviously missing from their
ancient formula would eventually be added to what was evolving into the Apostles' Creed.

The second reason is much more interesting and tells us
much about the purpose of this particular clause. As we saw in
the previous chapter, the Greek word now translated as
"almighty" is *pantokrator*, which literally means "all ruling." It
therefore refers not only to the power of God in abstract but also
to the activity of God in *all* things.

Challenges to Christian Doctrine

For the early church, this activity of God in all things was crucial, for there were those who denied it and in so doing changed

the entire meaning of the gospel. These were mainly the Gnostics, who claimed that all things spiritual were good but all things material were evil. A very influential teacher who lived in Rome precisely at the time when the Creed in its original form was composed held similar views. His name was Marcion, and he was the son of a bishop near the shores of the Black Sea. Marcion held that the God and Father of Jesus Christ is not the same as the secondary god who made the world—the Yahweh of Hebrew Scripture. Yahweh made the material world, perhaps out of ignorance or out of spite, but in any case against the wishes of the one true and highest God. In this material world human souls are now entrapped, and it was to free them that the true God sent Jesus. Marcion rejected any notion of continuity between creation and redemption, or between the faith of Abraham and the faith of Christians.[1] The mere title of "Christ" applied to Jesus should have sufficed to counteract such notions. But apparently Marcion took that title as part of Jesus' name and not as a declaration that Jesus is the fulfillment of the promises made to Israel. Later we shall see that Marcion's teachings had very serious consequences for the way people thought about Jesus, and that much of the Creed was composed as a way to counter the spread of Marcion's theories. For the present, however, let us look at what the word "almighty" would have meant for Christians in Rome in the second century.

"Almighty" in the Second Century

For a second century Christian—particularly one acquainted with the teaching of Marcion and of the Gnostics—the word *pantokrator* would be a statement not only about God but also about the world. To say that God is "all-ruling" implies both the power of God and the presence of that power in the "all" over which God rules.

It was precisely this that the Gnostics and Marcion denied. There is a good, spiritual creation, over which God rules. But then there is the material world, which is not only rebellious against God but can never be reconciled with God, for matter is by nature evil, and God only relates to the spiritual. This had further implications for most other aspects of Christian doctrine, for it meant that the Hebrew Scriptures—which constituted also the only Bible of Christians at the time—were not the revelation of the God and Father of Jesus Christ but of some other, lesser, and either ignorant or evil god. It also understood the human predicament to be that we are souls imprisoned in bodies and that if we can only rid ourselves of our bodies, and return to the purely spiritual realm, all will be well. But even more, it implied—as we shall see as we study the rest of the Creed—that Jesus did not really come in the flesh, which would have been an unacceptable mixing of the purely good with the intrinsically evil. Rather, he had a purely spiritual body, and he simply appeared to have a physical body and only seemed to die.

Faced with such teachings, when second-century Christians declared that God is "Almighty"—actually, *pantokrator* or "all-ruling"—they meant that God rules over both matter and spirit, that both matter and spirit are good, and that both matter and spirit are the object of the divine and loving purposes of salvation.

From "All-ruling" to "Omnipotent"

Strange as it may seem, Greek was the common language of most Christians in Rome in the second century. This was so because Christianity had come to Rome from the Greek-speaking eastern portion of the Empire, and therefore most of its converts were people with those connections. Thus, all surviving writings from the early church in Rome are in Greek. Soon, however, things began to change. Christianity spread to further reaches of the western section of the Empire, where Greek was not as common. This is why the earliest Christian writings in Latin do not come from Rome but from North Africa. In Rome itself, as the empire began to focus more and more on its western provinces, Greek tended to fall into disuse.

The old Roman creed—R—was now translated into Latin. In that translation, the Greek *pantokrator* (all-ruling) became *omnipotens* (omnipotent). To us today the difference may seem unimportant. But for Christians having to face the challenges of Marcionism and Gnosticism—as well as several other similar teachings—until well into the fourth century, the difference was crucial. To be omnipotent means to be able to do whatever one wishes, to have no limits to one's power. It refers primarily to God's own power and not so much to those things over which God's power rules. When it is understood in this way, God's omnipotence is quite problematic. Thus, there were medieval philosophers who asked whether God always does what is good (in which case God is limited by what is good) or whether whatever God does is good (in which case the good seems to be quite arbitrary).[2] Others asked whether God has the power to make a stone so big that even God cannot move it. Such speculations—which may seem ridiculous to some and quite disrespectful to others—are the result of a process whereby the human mind forgets its own limits. It poses something it cannot quite grasp—such as omnipotence—and then tries to draw conclusions from it.

This is not what the statement in the Creed is all about. The statement is an affirmation of God's power, yet not of God's power in general or in abstract but rather of God's power vis-à-vis the created order. Given the second century context and the theological challenges to Christian doctrine outlined above, the Creed is not so much an assertion of God's power in general as it is an assertion of God's power in relation to "all things"—again, *pantokrator*.

Creator of Heaven and Earth

When the Creed was translated into Latin, and *omnipotens* was substituted for *pantokrator*, the phrase was added, "Maker of heaven and earth." This was done in part to make the Creed similar to other statements of faith. But it was done also in order to remind believers of something that the Latin did not quite communicate, namely, that God's power extends over all things. The phrase "heaven and earth" is another way of saying "everything." The Nicene Creed explains it further by declaring that God is "Maker of heaven and earth, of all that is, seen and unseen." Within the context of what was being debated in Rome in the middle of the second century, this meant that God is the creator of both the physical and the spiritual, that matter is not evil in itself, that the spiritual in itself is no better than the material. Thus, in essence the phrase in the Creed is a safeguard against a false "spirituality" that is in truth spiritualism—as if only the spiritual were an object of God's concern and love.

Clearly this statement is just as important today as it was then. Today, as then, there are many doctrines and theories that tend to undervalue the material. There are many who think that God has to do only with "spiritual" matters, and that other issues—such as economics, ecology, and politics—have nothing to do with God or with religion. There are those within the church who think that God is concerned only with the salvation of souls and that the pain many bodies suffer, although unfortunate, is only a secondary matter. Then there are those who, dissatisfied with organized Christianity as they know it and rather distrustful of the church and its teaching, seek to rediscover ancient "wisdom" and supposedly mystical secrets known by the Mayas or the Chinese, whereby they hope to unlock the mysteries of the spiritual world. In many of our cities, there is even a revival of organized Gnosticism, where people are offered the arcane keys that will unlock the way into the spiritual world. All of these views tend to reject the notion that God is creator of heaven and earth and that all things—material and spiritual—are of value in the eyes of God.

On the other hand, there is in our time the opposite view. For many in our society, all that is important is the material. Blinded by the brilliance of modern technology and by the ease of life it offers, they live as if all that mattered were the material. Even though seldom expressing it in such terms, the basic premise of their worldview is that all mysteries can be solved by observation, experimentation, and science, and that all misery will eventually be solved by technology. For them also, the phrase "Maker of heaven and earth" may serve as a corrective. God is the creator not only of what we see and understand, that is, earth, but also of what we do not see and can never understand, that is, heaven. Beyond all our discoveries—important and valuable as they may be—there always remains the mystery of mysteries, the God whose creative action is not exhausted by the world we see, but goes far beyond it, to what we cannot even imagine.

Creation and Science

In recent times there has been much debate about creation and evolution. In this debate, many on both sides seem to have confused their roles and overstepped their boundaries. On the side of evolution, there is no doubt that disciplines such as paleontology and genetics can prove that species evolve from other species in a process that has been going on for millions of years. However, when scientists claim that such evolution is based on random occurrences they have gone beyond scientifically observable facts and wandered into the field of philosophy. On the side of creation, most who propose that it be taught as a possible scientific hypothesis forget that a scientific hypothesis is always capable of being proven wrong, and that they are therefore unwittingly opening the way for science to be the final arbiter on whether creation is true or not. Furthermore, many of those taking this position are not really defending the doctrine of creation but rather a particular account of creation they claim to find in the Bible, forgetting that in Genesis 1 and 2 there are two different accounts of creation. These two accounts, while agreeing that God is the creator of all things, do not agree on many details, such as the ordering of events. In one account, God makes animals first and then humans; in the other account, God makes the man first, then the animals, and finally the woman. Thus, what they claim to be the "biblical" account is in fact their own compilation and selection of those two accounts. The doctrine of creation is not about how God made the world; it is about this world and its inescapable dependence on God. Such a doctrine can never be proved or disproved by scientific research or analysis.

Unfortunately, these debates tend to obscure the significant contribution that the doctrine of creation has made to science. The scientific enterprise could not arise in a world populated and directed by a multitude of competing and even warring gods. If there is a god of rain and a god of death and in a particular year there is a lack of rain resulting in a famine, the explanation is obvious: The god of death has won over the god of rain. If next year the rain comes and the crops improve, this is now a sign that the god of rain has gained the upper hand. On the basis of such presuppositions, there is no need or even the possibility to try to find the causes of events or how they are linked with each other. The world and events in it are the capricious results of unknown powers that one can never understand. All one may do is to try to appease such powers, so that they may prove favorable. Within such a mental framework, science can scarcely develop.

The very notion of science—and even more the notion that scientific discoveries may be employed to alter events—requires that the world be viewed as a coherent whole. The ancient Greeks, while remaining polytheistic, were able to develop the rudiments of science because they believed that behind all the variety of the world, and even behind the multitude of gods, there was a single rational order— a *logos*, from which we derive our word "logic." With the advent of Christianity and the eventual prevalence of Judeo-Christian monotheism, which affirmed that the world is the creation of a single God, the foundation was laid for the systematic observation and exploration of the world, that is, for science, and for eventual attempts to influence nature and the outcome of events, that is, for technology. It is true that Christians did not always follow this path, and it is even true that at times organized Christianity has opposed scientific research and technological innovation. A famous example is the ecclesiastical opposition to the findings of Galileo. Today many who oppose evolution as if it were a religious doctrine, or as if evolution as a scientific hypothesis actually threatened Christian truth, seem to be following the same spirit of opposition to science and innovation. But even so, without the worldview derived from the Judeo-Christian doctrine of creation, or some other similar worldview, science and technology would not have developed as they have.

Creation and Nature

In summary, the doctrine of creation is not primarily about God but about the world. It is about the physical as well as about the spiritual world, about things we know and understand, and about things whose existence we may not even suspect. It is a declaration that God loves the entire world, not just some creatures in it. It is therefore a call to respect this world that God has made. It is not a call to return to some primitive state, when life was supposedly simpler, as if humankind had no business trying to alter the world. On the contrary, in both stories of creation in Genesis humanity is given a particular responsibility in the world. In one, it is given lordship—stewardship, management in God's name—over the rest of creation (Gen. 1:26). In the other, it is placed in the garden with the command to cultivate it (Gen. 2:15)—that is, to affect it in a positive way. The doctrine of creation does not mean that God made everything in its final form and that humankind is supposed to leave the world alone. It does mean that everything around us is important enough to have been created by God and therefore demands our respect and care.

I believe in God the Father Almighty, Maker of heaven and earth. And because I believe, I must love and respect this entire creation of which I am part, and in which God has placed me to carry out God's purpose. Ecological concern is not a passing fad, nor is it the possession of one political party or another; it springs out of the very doctrine of creation.

Questions for Discussion

1. In what ways can we affirm that God is "almighty" today?
2. What are the implications of affirming God as creator of all for our views of nature, humanity, and the church?
3. In the face of modern science, what is the importance of the affirmation that God is "Maker of heaven and earth"?

3

And in Jesus Christ His Only Son Our Lord

And in . . .

Three times in the Creed we affirm belief "in": in the Father, in Jesus Christ, and in the Holy Spirit. The reason for this is the original connection of the Creed with baptism, which resulted in the Creed having the same Trinitarian structure as the baptismal formula, "in the name of the Father, of the Son, and of the Holy Ghost." Here again, it is important to remember the distinction between believing *in* and believing *that*. The Creed affirms our belief *that* God is the creator of heaven and earth, *that* Jesus suffered under Pontius Pilate, and so forth. But it affirms our belief *in* God the Father, *in* Jesus Christ, and *in* the Holy Spirit. Thus, while not attempting to clarify all issues related with the doctrine of the Trinity, and even less to solve the mystery of the Trinity, the Creed affirms that doctrine, stating that it is *in* these three—the Father, the Son, and the Holy Spirit—that we live and move and have our being.

This is not the place to review the history of the doctrine of the Trinity. Suffice it to say here that this doctrine reflects the experience of Christians throughout the ages, and then to say a word about its significance for today. On the first point, it is clear that the experience of the early church, and of Christians since then, was one of encountering God in Jesus Christ. Jesus has always stood at the center of Christian faith, which has expressed this experience by affirming that he is divine. We know, however, that Jesus himself referred to God as his Father, and that when Jesus walked on the roads of Galilee God still reigned supreme over all. Thus, a distinction has to be made between Jesus as God and the Father as God. Likewise, Christians experience the presence of God within themselves and in the community of faith. This divine presence, which enables us to see and follow the will of God and to have communion with God, we call the Holy Spirit—or, in more traditional language, the Holy Ghost. Thus, Trinitarian doctrine affirms that the Father is God, that the Son is God, and that the Spirit is God; yet it also affirms that God is one.[1]

How the one is three has been the subject of much speculation, debate, and even dissension among Christians. Some have come to the conclusion that the very doctrine of the Trinity is irrelevant and should be abandoned. Were we to do that, we would find it difficult to understand and follow the faith of the New Testament and of Christians through the ages. Still, however, one must ask, what sense can we make out of the assertion that these three are different and yet are one God?

One way of looking at the Trinity and of seeing some of its relevance for today is to suggest that the Trinity itself leads us to review what we understand by oneness. God is one, but God is not one in solitary splendor. God is one in community, for even within the Godhead there is community. Brazilian theologian Leonardo Boff has expressed it as follows:

> God is Father, Son, and Holy Spirit in reciprocal communion. They coexist from all eternity; none is before or after, or superior or inferior, to the other. Each Person enwraps the others; all permeate one another and live in one another. This is the reality of Trinitarian communion, so infinite and deep that the divine Three are united and are therefore one sole God. The divine unity is communitarian because each Person is in communion with the other two. . . .
>
> The Persons are distinct . . . not in order to be separated but to come together and to be able to give themselves to one another.[2]

Something very similar to this was said much earlier by the author of the First Epistle of John: "God is love" (1 John 4:8). God is love and therefore loves us. But God is love in a much deeper sense. God is love because within the very Godhead there is love—love among the three divine persons. This in turn implies that when we speak of the oneness of God we do not mean only something similar to the oneness of a pebble or an apple; we speak also and above all of a oneness such as there is between true lovers. To say that "God is love" is to say that there is within the Godhead itself—and not only toward us—a love and a unity and a oneness similar to, but far beyond, the oneness of earthly lovers.

Therefore, the doctrine of the Trinity is not some idle speculation of feverish minds with nothing better to do. It stands at the very heart of the Christian understanding of God, and it is also the foundation on which Christians are to build community. There is a difference between oneness and aloneness that our highly individualistic society needs to rediscover and to ponder. God is one, but God is never alone. On the contrary, God is one in an eternal community of love. And the human community which we are invited to build—the community for which we were created—is a similar sort of community. It is a community of love, where each individual finds his or her identity in love for others. Our primary stance before the Trinity must not be to try to solve the mystery but rather to imitate the love!

Jesus Christ His Only Son Our Lord

There is a widespread notion that "Jesus" and "Christ" are two proper names. According to this view, "Jesus" is the name of the man from Nazareth who was crucified under Pontius Pilate, and "Christ" is the name of Jesus in his heavenly function. Thus, some people speak of "the Jesus of history and the Christ of faith." However, "Jesus" is a name, and "Christ" is an adjective or a past participle meaning "anointed." In fact, *Christos* is the Greek equivalent of the Hebrew *Messiah*, which means "anointed."

In ancient society—and certainly in the Old Testament—people were anointed as a sign of being set apart and consecrated for a particular role or function. In Israel, priests were anointed—as were kings, which is the reason why David is often called "God's anointed."

Over the centuries and amid a history of exile and oppression, Israel came to look forward to an anointed one—but not anointed merely to be one more along the long list of priests, not even as a king who would be subservient to Rome or to some other foreign power. The anointed one or messiah for which Israel longed would restore and even surpass the kingdom of David, would destroy the enemies of God and of Israel, and would bring about a new order of peace and justice.

When calling Jesus "the Christ"—the Anointed One or Messiah— the early church was affirming both its continuity with Israel and its conviction that the hope of Israel had been fulfilled in Jesus. For obvious reasons, many Jews objected to this. But so did those Christians who, like Marcion, claimed that the religion of Israel was all wrong and that Jesus and his message had nothing to do with it. In the Christian community in Rome, where the Creed was taking shape in the second century, the doctrines of Marcion were a very real threat, and therefore the Creed makes it clear that Jesus is the fulfillment of the promises made to Israel by the God of Israel—who is none other than the God of Christians, "Maker of heaven and earth."

His Only Son

One can detect a similar purpose in the often overlooked phrase "his only Son." For us today, what is often debated is whether Jesus is indeed a person as special as is implied in calling him "the Son of God." For the first Christians reciting the Creed, it was equally important to make clear that Jesus is the Son of the God who is "Father Almighty, Maker of heaven and earth." Jesus is the son of the Creator and not of an alien God. He comes to fulfill the purposes of the Creator, because creation is good, and because God, the Father of Jesus, loves creation.

At first this may seem scarcely relevant for us, nineteen centuries after the earliest form of the Creed was composed. Marcion and his teachings are no longer with us. So why insist on Jesus being the Christ and on his being the Son of the God who has created all things? Because, among other things, we need this doctrine in order to clarify the relationship between Christianity and the faith of Israel and, by extension, between Christians and Jews.

We frequently hear that the great difference between Christianity and Judaism is precisely on this issue of the Messiah—whether or not

Jesus is the Messiah, whether or not the Messiah has already come.
There are indeed significant differences here, and even a casual reader
of the New Testament will note that this was one of the main points of
contention between those Jews who accepted Christianity, such as Peter
and Paul, and those who did not. But there is another side of the coin—
and an important one: In declaring Jesus to be the Messiah, Christianity
affirms its continuity with the faith of Israel, and Christians acknowledge our debt to Abraham and his descendants. During its early years,
Christianity had to carve out and define its identity vis-à-vis traditional
Judaism. This led many Christians to emphasize and even exaggerate
the difference between the two. In later centuries, after Christianity had
become the official religion of most of Europe, documents and notions
from an earlier time and a different context fed into anti-Jewish senti-
ments, thus leading to discrimination and pogroms—and eventually to
the Holocaust.

For this reason it is important for us to realize that when we call
Jesus "the Christ" we are claiming and acknowledging that there is a
connection between our faith and that of our Jewish neighbors. We
may disagree on many points of doctrine and of practice, but if the
faith delivered to Abraham and his descendants is false, we have no
right and no reason to call Jesus "the Christ."

The Creed does not say only that Jesus is the Son of the God who
created heaven and earth; it says also that this relationship is extraor-
dinary. Jesus is "his only Son." This point will be made more force-
fully in the phrase we shall study in the next chapter, "conceived by
the Holy Spirit, born of the Virgin Mary."[3] Whatever we find in that
other phrase is in part an explanation or expansion of what is already
being said here: Jesus is "his *only* Son."

Our Lord

We say "our Lord" with such ease that it is difficult for us to see what
a radical statement it was for Christians in the second century—and
what a radical statement it should still be. The title of "Lord" (*Kyrios*)
was claimed by Emperor Domitian late in the first century. It meant
that he was the supreme ruler and that no one could challenge or even
rival his authority. Domitian's attitude, manifested in the title itself but

also in a number of other actions, led to the persecution of both Christians and Jews, who insisted that God was the true Lord, far above Domitian or any other ruler. The book of Revelation attests to the tension this brought to the church and to the temptation of many to yield before imperial claims to absolute power.

After Domitian, most emperors claimed this title for themselves. Whenever a rival aspirant to the throne appeared—usually among the legions—the first thing his supporters did was to burn incense before his image and declare him to be lord.

Thus, when Christians dared call Jesus "our Lord," they were uttering subversive and perhaps even seditious statements. They were claiming that there was another Lord besides—and even above—the emperor. This was not tolerated. Christians were ordered to burn incense before the emperor's image and to reject Jesus as "Lord." Because they refused to do this, many were tortured and put to death. They were called "martyrs," that is, "witnesses," because they had given witness to the lordship of Christ even at the price of death. In one of the many accounts of the acts of these martyrs, one of them is urged by the judge, "You are to obey the decrees of the emperors and caesars," to which the martyr replies, "I care only for the law of God. This I have learned. This I obey. For it I am to die. In it I wish to finish my life. Beside it there is no other law."[4]

Our Lord?

Time has passed, and it would seem that the claim that Jesus Christ is Lord has become commonplace and has lost most of its edge. We tend to think that the lordship of Christ is a purely religious statement, or at best a statement about how we are to conduct our daily lives. We tend to think that this is one of many commitments we have and that it exists side-by-side with our commitments to: family, nation, church, political philosophy, political party, and so forth. But the lordship of Christ, properly understood, questions or at least limits every other lordship and every other allegiance. When the early Christians declared, "I believe in . . . Jesus Christ . . . our Lord," they were not making an innocuous statement. Nor are we. We are saying that our ultimate commitment is not to family, not to nation, not to church, but to him. We are rejecting every absolute nationalism. We are rejecting any other unconditional allegiance. Otherwise, he is not truly "our Lord," but one more among our many lords.

This became quite clear for many Christians in Germany under Nazi rule. The government demanded complete and unconditional loyalty. Nationalism, as understood by Hitler and his followers, was an excuse for any and all things. The organized church was made subservient to the state, acquiesced to what the government was doing, and even claimed that it was done in the name of Christianity. But then there were some who understood what they had been affirming throughout their lives, that Jesus Christ is *our Lord.* A number of these gathered in Barmen and issued a declaration in which they bravely stated:

> Jesus Christ, as he is attested to us in Holy Scripture, is the one Word of God which we have to hear and which we have to trust and obey in life and in death.
>
> We reject the false doctrine, as though the church could and would have to acknowledge as a source of its proclamation, apart from and besides this one Word of God, still other events and powers, figures and truths, as God's revelation.[5]

This was no idle statement, and many of those who affirmed it were persecuted and killed by the government.

What do we mean today when we declare that we believe in Jesus Christ our Lord? What are we denying? What are we risking? These are questions worth pondering as we repeat words for which so many have suffered.

Questions for Discussion

1. Why is the doctrine of the Trinity vital for Christian belief?
2. What is the significance of affirming that Jesus Christ is the "only Son" of the Father?
3. In what ways can we affirm that Jesus Christ is Lord today?

4

Who Was Conceived by the Holy Spirit, Born of the Virgin Mary

A Common Misunderstanding

Most people today, when they hear or repeat the words in the Creed "who was conceived by the Holy Spirit, born of the Virgin Mary" interpret them in the light of modern biology. We know that conception comes from the union of two cells, one from the father and one from the mother. In that union, genes are combined from both parents, thus determining the inherited traits that the new person will have—half from the male and half from the female. On the basis of this biological understanding, they then interpret the words of the Creed to mean that Jesus is half human and half divine.

This is very different from the way people understood conception in ancient times. As the ancients thought of it, conception and birth were the result of a male seed being planted in the womb, much as a grain of wheat is planted in the ground. The presence in the offspring of traits similar to its mother's was explained much as one would explain the manner in which the soil affects the plant: The womb was the mold in which the offspring was shaped. The mother did not contribute an ovum—of whose existence the ancients were unaware—but only the nourishment that made it possible for the seed to grow. Were we then to interpret the words of the Creed in biological terms, according to the biology of the times, we would come to a very different conclusion than we do when we apply our current biological knowledge.

But the purpose of these words is not to explain Jesus' biological origin. It is rather to make two central affirmations about him: first, that his birth was something special; second, that his birth was real.

A Special Birth

There is in the Old Testament a common thread that may help us understand the importance of what the Creed says about the birth of Jesus. This is the theme of the barren woman, which was quite common in early Christian interpretation of the Hebrew Scriptures. In them, one reads repeatedly that when a child was needed to continue the line of the patriarchs, or to perform a special task, that child was the result of God's action. Its mother was a barren woman who conceived by divine intervention.

This is the story of Abraham and Sarah, and the birth of their son Isaac is well known. What we tend to forget is that the story is not only about how God chose Abraham to be the father of many, but also about how God chose Sarah. This is not so strange, since Abraham and Sarah themselves showed the same masculine bias. When Sarah could not conceive, they decided that in order for the promise to be fulfilled, that Abraham would be "the father of many nations," Abraham had to lie with Sarah's servant Hagar. But God would have none of this. God had chosen both Abraham and Sarah, and it was their unexpected child Isaac that would be the bearer of the promise.

The story of Isaac is similar. Rebekah is chosen to be Isaac's wife, but she is barren. So "Isaac prayed to the LORD for his wife, because she was barren; and the LORD granted his prayer, and his wife Rebekah conceived" (Gen. 25:21).

Then comes the story of Jacob, the son of Isaac and Rebekah, and his wives and concubines. Jacob marries Leah and Rachel, and the latter is the wife of his heart, but she cannot conceive until "God remembered Rachel, and God heeded her and opened her womb" (Gen. 30:22). The result of this unexpected but welcome pregnancy is Joseph, who would save his family in a time of famine and find them a place in Egypt.

Isaac, Jacob, and Joseph are not the only children of previously barren women. The same is true of other great figures in the history of Israel, such as Samson, Samuel, and John the Baptist.

Male Jewish Writers – Virgin-type of woman in the old testament Sara, Naomi, Ruth (Barren!) (line of David)

For an agricultural people such as ancient Israel, the fertility of land, flocks, and people was of primary importance. If the harvest failed, or if the flock did not reproduce, there was famine. If a family had no sons to support it when the older generation was unable to continue working, the result was poverty and even starvation. Furthermore, if a couple failed to reproduce, this was usually seen as the woman's fault. As a result, for a woman not to be able to conceive was considered a serious flaw and even a curse. This is why there are in the Bible so many stories of rivalries among wives and concubines, each trying to outdo the others in fertility, and often the barren one feeling inadequate.

Both Israel and the various peoples surrounding it believed that fertility was a divine gift. It is God (or the gods) that keeps nature on its course, and an important part of that course is the fertility of land, flocks, and families. Yet Israel's faith went beyond the mere upkeep of the cycle of nature. God certainly does that, but God also has a purpose in history. God intervenes in the cycles of nature in order to carry forth that purpose.

The theme of the barren women who conceive then has theological significance. They conceive as a sign that the children born of their pregnancies are not merely the result of natural forces, but are conceived and born because of a specific act of God, so that God's purposes may be fulfilled.[1]

This theme continues in the New Testament with the story of Elizabeth and her son John the Baptist. Elizabeth and Zechariah are a saintly couple who obey all the commandments of God. "But they had no children, because Elizabeth was barren, and both were getting on in years" (Luke 1:7). While serving at the sanctuary, Zechariah has a vision that Elizabeth will conceive and bear a son, and he is also told that his son has a special place in God's plans, "for he will be great in the sight of the Lord" (1:15).

When Elizabeth's pregnancy is well advanced, her relative Mary is also visited by an angel and told that she too will conceive and that her son will also be special: "He will be great, and will be called the Son of the Most High, and the Lord God will give to him the throne of his ancestor David. He will reign over the house of Jacob forever, and of his kingdom there will be no end" (1:32–33).

Luke makes it clear that just as Jesus is the culmination of the hope of Israel, Mary is the culmination of the theme of the barren woman who conceived by divine intervention. The song he puts on the lips of Mary, the Magnificat (1:47–55), is patterned after the song of Hannah (1 Sam. 2:1–10), another barren woman who conceives and bears a child with a specific purpose in God's plans—Samuel.

For early Christians, the virgin birth was simply the culmination of the ancient theme of the barren woman who conceives. What is intended by it is not to explain Jesus' biological origin but rather to make it plain that just as in past times God raised leaders for Israel out of barren women who conceived by divine intervention, now the barren woman par excellence—a virgin—conceives by divine intervention ("by the Holy Spirit"). Moreover, the child she will bear will be not only exceptional but unequalled—the Son of the Most High, whose kingdom will have no end.

A Real Birth

In the words of the Creed, however, the emphasis lies not only on the unique nature of this birth but also on its reality. Strange as it may seem to us today, during its early centuries Christianity faced its greatest challenge, not from those who claimed that Jesus was a mere man but rather from those who claimed that he was not really human—that he was a purely spiritual being who seemed to be human but was not. While there were many who held such views, Marcion in particular denied that Jesus was born. Commenting on Marcion's views, North African theologian Tertullian wrote:

> Marcion, in order that he might deny the flesh of Christ, denied also His nativity; or else he denied His flesh in order that he might deny His nativity; because, of course, he was afraid that His nativity and His flesh bore mutual testimony to each other's reality, since there is no nativity without flesh, and no flesh without nativity. . . . He who represented the flesh of Christ to be imaginary was equally able to pass off His nativity as a phantom; so that the virgin's conception, and pregnancy, and child-bearing, and then the whole course of her infant too, would have to be regarded as imaginary.[2]

Note that here the virgin's conception serves to prove, not the divinity of Jesus as we might surmise, but rather his humanity. What Marcion could not accept is not that Jesus was born of a virgin, but simply the fact that he was *born*. On this score, one could even suggest that, given the anti-Marcionite nature of the Creed, the word "virgin" in the phrase "born of the Virgin Mary" should be translated as "born of Mary the virgin," for it is intended as a way to refer to a particular woman more than as a way to underscore her virginity.

Whatever the case may be, there is no doubt that "born of the Virgin Mary" emphasized both the uniqueness and the reality of the birth of Jesus—the uniqueness making him the Lord of all and the reality making him like one of us.

Later Developments

Unfortunately, as time went by and the challenge of Marcion and others like him faded away, the theme of the virgin birth became the object of much pious speculation that now centered on Mary more than on Jesus. Mary's virginity in itself, rather than the one who was born of her, became the center of attention. In order to safeguard that virginity, she must never have lain with Joseph, even after the birth of Jesus—who certainly must have had no siblings! Then her virginity came to be understood in such terms that the birth of Jesus could not have been "through the natural door," for this would violate his mother's virginity.[3] Eventually this would lead to the claim that Mary herself was conceived without sin, that she was assumed directly into heaven, and even that she is Coredemptrix with Jesus.

Ironically, what all of this has done is to open the way to precisely the view of Christ that the Creed sought to avoid in affirming the virgin birth. Marcion and others like him could not admit that Jesus was born, because a birth would prove that he was indeed fully human. A birth is a very messy thing, and the Creed affirms that Jesus underwent it. A birth is a sign of powerlessness, for the newly born is totally dependent on others, and the Creed affirms that Jesus underwent it. Over against this, all the speculation making the birth of Jesus clean and unreal plays into the hands of Marcion and his views, and denies the full humanity of Jesus, which the Creed is trying to safeguard.

Once again, over against such views, the Creed affirms both that the birth of Jesus is unique and that it is real. It affirms that the one who was conceived by the Holy Spirit and born of the Virgin Mary was as human and as unique as his birth indicates.

Questions for Discussion

1. Why is affirming the special nature of Jesus' birth important theologically?
2. Is the virgin birth an indispensable part of Christian belief? Why or why not?
3. Why has the Christian church stressed that Jesus is both divine and human?

5

Suffered under Pontius Pilate,
Was Crucified, Dead, and Buried

Why Pontius Pilate?

When I first heard the Creed, I wondered why there was in it such animosity against Pontius Pilate. Why single him out, when so many others were at least as guilty as he was—Judas, Herod, the mob, the Roman soldiers? After all, all that he did was to withhold judgment, while others rushed to it. He even made a weak attempt to save Jesus, yet the Creed singles him out. Why?

The answer is quite simple. The name of Pontius Pilate does not appear in the Creed in order to lay blame, but simply as a date. The Creed would not date the suffering of Jesus "in the year X," for such dating had not appeared yet. At the time, most dating was based either on counting years "from the foundation of Rome," or on who happened to be ruling at a particular time. We find examples of this in well-known passages both in the Old Testament and in the New. For instance, in the Old: "In the year that King Uzziah died, I saw the Lord sitting on a throne" (Isa. 6:1). And in the New: "This was the first registration and was taken while Quirinius was governor of Syria" (Luke 2:2).

Why did the Creed give such importance to dating the events to which it refers? Simply to show that these were not eternal recurring myths, as in many other religions of the time. In Egypt, for instance, the annual flooding of the Nile was explained by the myth of Isis and Osiris. According to this myth, the god Osiris was killed and dismembered by his brother Seth, who scattered the remains all over Egypt. Osiris's wife Isis gathered the various parts of her husband's body and brought him back to life. But his genitalia she could not recover, for they had fallen into the Nile. This is the reason why the river floods every year, bringing to the land the fertility of Osiris. Other religions explained the annual cycle of death in winter and resurgence in spring with similar myths in which a divine being dies and is brought back to life.

Now the Creed is about to state faith in a divine being who died and was brought back to life. This sounds very much like many of the surrounding religions of fertility. How did early Christians avoid that? By making it clear that the Creed is not referring to a recurring cycle but to a series of datable historical events. Osiris and the various fertility gods die and rise again every year. Jesus Christ died and rose again only once, but this once is good enough for all the ages.

Using the name of Pontius Pilate as a way of dating the events of the passion of Jesus seems to have been fairly common from an early date—and not only in Rome, where the Creed had its origin. Early in the second century the bishop of Antioch, Ignatius, wrote seven letters to various churches. In those letters he shows that he is deeply concerned over theories and doctrines that deny the true humanity of Jesus. He exhorts his readers to "be absolutely certain of the birth, passion, and resurrection of the Lord, which took place under the rule of Pontius Pilate."[1] A few decades later, roughly at the same time when the Creed was taking its early shape in Rome, Justin Martyr repeatedly used the same method for dating the passion and resurrection of Jesus.[2]

In the fourth century, Rufinus explained this particular clause in the Creed as follows:

> Those who have bequeathed the Creed to us were very wise in emphasizing the actual time when all these things took place, so that the firmness of the tradition be well established, and there be no danger of uncertainty or vagueness.[3]

This was particularly important, since there were those who turned the story of Jesus into a myth about eternal realities and thus felt free to mix and join them with the various myths of the time, simply adding Jesus to the list of their gods.

Was Crucified

That Jesus "was crucified" is the most astonishing admission of the entire Creed. We tend to think of the "scandal of the cross" as consisting in the notion that God can suffer. This is indeed part of it. But for Christians in the Roman Empire the "scandal" was much worse than that. The cross of Jesus was not unique. On the contrary, crucifixion was the common way in which the Romans punished the worst criminals, particularly those of the lower classes, for Roman citizens had the right to be decapitated instead of crucified. In fact, on occasion thousands of people were crucified at the same time, with their limp, hanging bodies lining the highways.

Crucifixion was certainly a painful death. The person was hung on a cross in a position that made even breathing difficult, and was left there to die of exposure. Sometimes nails were used, and sometimes the convicted criminal was simply hung with ropes. In any case it was a prolonged, agonizing death. But even more than painful, crucifixion was humiliating. The one to be executed was striped naked, and the mockery that the Gospels relate was not unusual. Once the person died, the body was often left hanging there, to be eaten by birds and eventually to break into pieces, with dogs and other scavengers picking up the bones. Although the body of Jesus was taken off the cross out of respect for a Jewish religious festival, his crucifixion was no less humiliating than any other.

For those early Christians to affirm that their Lord was crucified would be as scandalous as for someone today to affirm faith in a person who died in the electric chair. What the Creed actually affirms is that the Lord—the *Kyrios* whom Christians follow even in preference to the emperor—died like a common criminal under Roman law.

Such a declaration of faith would have been not only scandalous and even ridiculous but also subversive. What Christians were actually saying in reciting this Creed was that Roman law had erred in crucifying Jesus. The empire killed him as a seditious man claiming to be "King of the Jews," but it had actually crucified the king of the universe!

Imagine yourself a loyal official in the Roman Empire. What would you think about a group of people who claimed that their God was the "ruler of all," who followed a man crucified as a common and seditious criminal, and who referred to him by the title of "Lord," a title claimed by the emperor himself?

Once again, the Creed was not a mere list of innocuous beliefs. It was a clear statement of what it means to believe *in* this God who rules the universe, *in* this Son who is crucified as a common criminal, and *in* the Spirit who makes believers participants in the death and resurrection of that convicted criminal.

Suffered . . . Crucified, Dead, and Buried

Those in Christianity's early centuries who denied the humanity of Jesus were many, and they belonged to a number of different schools, each with its own particular set of doctrines. What they had in common was the notion that Jesus, being the Savior, could not have been truly human—and more specifically, that he could not have had a real physical body like ours. Since they claimed that the body of Christ was unreal, that it was a mere appearance, they soon were called "Docetists," from a Greek word meaning "to appear" or "to seem."

Over against such views, Christians insisted on the reality of the incarnation of God in a true, full, human being. Ignatius was so concerned over this matter that he felt compelled to stress the reality of the physical life of Jesus:

> Stop your ears if someone comes to speak to you against Jesus Christ, who is descended from the line of David and is the son of Mary; who was truly born, and truly ate and drank; who was truly persecuted under Pontius Pilate, was truly crucified and died in view of all who inhabit heaven, earth, and under the earth. Who also truly rose again.[4]

And in another passage, closing with some humor, he says:

> For the Lord suffered all these things for us and for our salvation; and he truly suffered it, just as he truly rose himself from the dead; and not, as some unbelievers claim, that he only appeared to suffer. They are the ones who are mere appearance!

And just as they think, so will it happen to them, that they will remain incorporeal and demonic beings.[5]

It is important to understand this, for in recent times there has been much discussion about a number of "gospels" that purport to tell the true story of Jesus. Most of these gospels are not only much later than the four we now have in the New Testament, but they are also gnostic, or at least docetic, for they present Jesus as not fully human and not bound by the physical needs of any human body. In the *Gospel of James*, for instance, Jesus is not really born. Joseph goes out looking for a midwife and brings her to the cave where Mary awaits. But upon arriving at the cave, Joseph and the midwife are blinded by a bright cloud that covers everything. When the cloud disappears and they are able to look into the cave, Jesus is already at his mother's breast.[6] Others claim that when Simon of Cyrene was called upon to share the burden of the cross, Jesus traded places with him, so that it was actually Simon who suffered; Jesus simply walked away. Still others make the point that Jesus did not need to eat, for his body was nourished with heavenly food. A frequent trait among the various groups that produced some of these gospels is also the reversal of the values of the Old Testament. We have already seen that according to Marcion the God of the Old Testament is not the one true God, and all his creation is to be rejected. There was also a group called the "Cainites," because for them Cain was the great hero in Genesis, and another called the "Ophites," because their hero was the serpent (Greek, *ophis*). The recently published *Gospel of Judas*, as well as several other texts, make of Judas the hero, who was told by Jesus to betray him. Even though the press gave wide coverage to the *Gospel of Judas*, it says nothing that was not already rejected by the early church and little that modern scholars did not know.

The reason why the Creed stresses the suffering, death, and burial of Jesus is to counteract the various theories circulating at the time, to the effect that Jesus did not really suffer and did not really die, for his body was heavenly and incorruptible—or, in the view of some, his body was not even real. Again, the Creed is not attempting to summarize all of Christian doctrine. Because what was most debated at the time was the person of Jesus and his true humanity, the Creed stresses the historical birth, suffering, and death of Jesus.

Some Reflections for Today

When one looks at what the Creed says about Jesus, one may well be astounded that the early Christians were able to declare with such openness that he was not a respectable character by Roman standards, nor even by Jewish standards, which considered crucifixion a curse from God (Deut. 21:23; Gal. 3:13). They made no bones about declaring that he was killed by the established authorities as a seditious criminal, and that they still considered this criminal their Lord. As a result they were mocked, persecuted, and killed.

Reflecting on this, one cannot help but be struck at the contrast between those early Christians and many Christians today, whose main concern seems to be that their faith be equated with common decency and that society at large somehow acknowledge and respect the Lord. In the United States, many even feel that society at large has declared war on Christianity, and therefore speak of a vast conspiracy to eradicate all vestiges of Christianity from the surrounding culture—a conspiracy that includes no longer saying "Merry Christmas," teaching evolution in schools, and giving other religions equal rights with Christianity. In contrast with these attitudes, more liberal Christians say that there is no such conspiracy, and that the reason why Christianity is losing prestige in society at large is the narrow-mindedness of conservative Christians.

Our second century sisters and brothers who recited the Creed in its early form would disagree with both positions. First of all, they would reject the common liberal view, declaring that there is indeed a conspiracy against God and against the gospel. But they would also reject the more conservative view that this conspiracy is a recent invention on the part of people seeking to destroy the moral and religious fiber of society. They would say rather that the conspiracy has always existed. It existed from the beginning, as sin entered creation, thus requiring the saving work of Jesus. It existed as Jesus walked on earth, thus leading to his suffering and death. And it existed in the second century, when Christians lived under the constant threat of persecution. They would say, with Paul, that "our struggle is not against enemies of blood and flesh, but against the rulers, against the authorities, against the cosmic powers of this present darkness, against the spiritual forces of evil in the heavenly places" (Eph. 6:12).

Furthermore, many of our sisters and brothers in other lands today—in lands where the witness of the church seems to be more powerful and effective than in ours—would agree with them and with Paul. They have no support from a society that either opposes or ignores them. They are often considered bad citizens of their nations and even traitors to their culture and heritage. Being a Christian is nothing to be proud of in the society in which they live. Yet they choose to be Christians, not because it is respectable or because Christianity enjoys support from the culture or the state, but out of sheer faith and conviction. No wonder their testimony bears such fruit!

Most of us, in contrast, seem to think that what is most important is the prestige of our faith. Many conservatives act as if prayer in schools, the teaching of creationism, and the banning of gay marriage would show that our faith is still at the center of our culture. They are convinced that, as Christians, they should first of all obey the law of the land and then condemn any who do not obey it, such as illegal immigrants. Many liberals seem to think that our faith would be more respectable were we to prove more enlightened, accepting the new mores of our society and raising no fuss over the changing environment. They are convinced that society as it exists is generally good and quite compatible with Christian faith. But the Creed, and the experience of early Christians expressed in it, tells us otherwise. The one in whom we believe is a convicted criminal, not a respected religious leader. His followers should not expect to be particularly respected, and they should not expect society to support their faith. What happened to Jesus Christ under Pontius Pilate continues happening to his most faithful followers in every age and in any society.

All of this brings us back to the issue of what it is we are saying when we declare that we believe *in* God the Father Almighty, and *in* Jesus Christ his only Son our Lord, and *in* the Holy Spirit. What we are saying is that it is in this triune God—the God Almighty who suffers in Jesus Christ and who comes to us in the Spirit—that we build our lives, that it is *in* this God that we not only believe but also exist.

Questions for Discussion

1. What is the significance of recognizing that Jesus was crucified "under Pontius Pilate"?
2. Why does the Creed emphasize Jesus' suffering, death, and burial?
3. What are the implications for today from what this article of the Creed says about Jesus Christ?

6

He Descended to the Dead

A Slight Disagreement

If you visit different churches and recite the Creed with them, you will note that most of them—Catholic, Anglican, Lutheran, Reformed—include the statement that "he descended to the dead" or "he descended into hell," while some, particularly those of the Wesleyan tradition, do not. The reason for this discrepancy is not really a theological difference or disagreement; it is only a disagreement as to what version of the Creed to employ. John Wesley, being a patristic scholar, knew that it was not included in most creeds until a relatively late date—the fourth century in one particular case, but generally the sixth to the eighth centuries. By the beginning of the ninth it was included in the official version of the Apostles' Creed.

Even so, Wesley—while recognizing that the phrase itself was a late addition to the Creed—affirmed the doctrine. In "A Letter to a Roman Catholic," he summarizes part of his faith in words that are clearly a paraphrase of the Creed and that include the descent into hell:

> I believe he suffered inexpressible pains both of body and soul, and at last death, even the death of the cross, at the time that Pontius Pilate governed Judea, under the Roman Emperor; that his body was then laid in the grave, *and his soul went to the place of separate spirits*; that the third day he rose again from the dead; that he ascended into heaven; where he remains in the midst of the throne of God, in the highest power and glory, as Mediator till the end of

He Descended to the Dead   49

the world, as God to all eternity; that, in the end, he will come down from heaven, to judge every man according to his works; both those who shall be then alive, and all who have died before that day.[1]

To say that the earlier version of the Creed—R and its first successors—did not include this phrase does not mean that Christians at the time did not believe in the descent into hell. On the contrary, many early Christian writers did affirm it; therefore, no matter whether we recite this line in the Creed or not, we do well to explore its meaning.

The Meaning of the Descent

There are several different meanings attached to this clause, all of them probably true at least in part. First, there is the notion of descent itself. As one reads the Creed from the declaration that Jesus was born to this point, the movement is clearly downward. The eternal Son of God descends to earth through birth, and at his death continues descending to the lower places—which is the original meaning of the word *infernus*. This establishes a marked contrast with the next clause, where we declare that he rose again from the dead, ascended into heaven, and sits at the right hand of God. Thus viewed, much of what the Creed says about Jesus is parallel to what Paul says in his famous hymn in Philippians 2, that Jesus, "though he was in the form of God, did not regard equality with God as something to be exploited, but emptied himself, taking the form of a slave, being born in human likeness. And being found in human form, he humbled himself and became obedient to the point of death—even death on a cross" (Phil. 2:6–8). The parallelism will continue as we move along the Creed, where we shall find that the one who descended is also the one who has ascended and is exalted, as Paul declares in the rest of his hymn.

Second, the descent into hell is the final affirmation of the real death of Jesus. It was a traditional Jewish belief that the souls of the dead went to a place below the earth. According to the Pharisees, they were there to await the final resurrection. Thus, in his treatise *On the Soul,* Tertullian explains that all souls go to the underworld at the point of death, and that Jesus therefore went to the underworld because he was really dead. Jesus was fully human, and therefore "he fully complied [with the meaning of a human death] by remaining in Hades in the form and condition of a dead man."[2]

Third, it was thought that Jesus descended into the place of the dead in order to preach to those who lived before Jesus and who were imprisoned in the place of the dead awaiting the presence and preaching of Jesus to them. This notion appears in 1 Peter, where we read that Christ "was put to death in the flesh, but made alive in the spirit, in which also he went and made a proclamation to the spirits in prison, who in former times did not obey, when God waited patiently in the days of Noah" (1 Pet. 3:18–20). Although in 1 Peter the reference is only to those who lived in the time of Noah, this passage was sometimes employed to explain how Abraham and his descendants who lived before the time of Jesus could be saved. The common view during the Middle Ages was that when Jesus descended into hell he preached to all who had lived before him, thus giving them an opportunity for salvation. According to tradition, the apostles had preached to every nation, so that those living after Jesus who did not believe had been given an opportunity and failed to make use of it. Thus, by descending into hell and there preaching to those who had lived before him, Jesus gave them a fair opportunity for salvation.

A Fourth Meaning

The fourth meaning traditionally attributed to the descent of Jesus into hell has to do with his victory over the powers of evil. In this view, the saving work of Jesus consists primarily in defeating those powers and thus undoing their hold on humankind. In order to do this, Jesus descends to the very abode of evil—hell—and there, through his resurrection, defeats it. This view also finds an echo in the New Testament, where we are told in Ephesians that the saving work of Christ is seen in what the Old Testament declares, that "when he ascended on high he made captivity itself a captive" (Eph. 4:8, quoting Ps. 68:18). The epistle goes on to explain the meaning of this in a parenthetical phrase that seems to include the descent of Jesus into hell: "When it says, 'He ascended,' what does it mean but that he had also descended into the lower parts of the earth? He who descended is the same one who ascended far above all the heavens" (Eph. 4:9–10).

This may well lead us to think of the saving work of Christ in a different fashion than we usually do. For most of us, the traditional understanding of the human predicament and of the work of Christ in response to it is couched in terms of sin as a debt owed to God. We have all heard evangelistic sermons whose outline is roughly that (1) God created us and gave us freedom to obey or to disobey the divine law; (2) we have broken God's law, and therefore now have a debt to pay, much as a criminal has a debt to pay to society; (3) since it is owed by humanity, this debt has to be paid by a human being; (4) since it is infinite, it can only be paid by an infinite being, namely, God; (5) thus, God becomes human in order to pay our debt; (6) this human, Jesus, dies on the cross, which is a payment for all the sins of humankind; (7) in order to benefit from this payment of our debt, we are to accept and confess Jesus. Traditional as all of this may seem to us, it is not the most common understanding of the gospel in the early church—indeed, it does not appear in its full expression until late in the eleventh century, and even then was resisted by more traditional theologians.[3]

In contrast to this portrayal, there were many in the early church who saw the human predicament as a bondage to sin and to the devil, and therefore the work of Christ as a victory over them—a victory that then frees us to be what God intends us to be. From this perspective, what Ephesians means by declaring that Jesus "made captivity itself a captive" is precisely that he conquered and made captive the one who had held sway over us. In a similar vein, early Christians referred to the work of Christ as having "killed death." Thus, we find many early Christian writers referring to the work of Christ as a liberation from the powers of evil and as the beginning of the new humanity free from those powers. One of them is Irenaeus, who wrote in the second half of the second century:

> For he fought and conquered; . . . and through obedience doing away with disobedience completely: for he bound the strong man, and set free the weak, and endowed his own handiwork with salvation, by destroying sin.[4]

He then continues explaining that this required for Jesus to be both divine and human, although his explanation is different from the notion that Jesus had to be human in order to pay our debt, and divine in order to make his payment sufficient:

> He caused man to cleave to and to become one with God. For unless man had overcome the enemy of man, the enemy would not have been legitimately vanquished. And again: unless it had been God who had freely given salvation, we could never have possessed it securely.[5]

Viewed within the context of this theology, the descent into hell—no matter whether part of the Creed or not—is much more than the mere consequence of death. It is also more than an opportunity for Jesus to preach to those who were awaiting his coming. It is an essential part of his work of salvation, for it is through this descent that Jesus enters the very headquarters of evil, in order to destroy its power.

This in turn means that the significance of the descent—and even of the cross—can only be understood in the light of the resurrection. Through the incarnation, the cross, and the descent into hell, in which the devil seemed to be victorious, Jesus made his way into the very headquarters of evil, there to defeat it.

If they were writing today, I can well imagine some of those early Christian writers saying that in the incarnation God entered a world and a humanity where evil held sway, that at the cross the devil seemed to have conquered, took home a neatly wrapped package that seemed his greatest prize, and smugly locked it in his safe. But the package was a time bomb—if the reader will forgive such a militaristic image. And on the third day . . .

Questions for Discussion

1. Do you believe that the phrase "he descended to the dead" or "he descended into hell" is an important part of the Creed? Why or why not?

2. Which view of the meaning of the descent into hell is most meaningful to you? Why?
3. In what ways today do we see the powers of evil as destroyed or overcome by the Christ who "descended into hell"?

7

On the Third Day He Rose Again

He Is Risen!

What is expressed in these few words is the very crux of the Christian faith. One may debate exactly what one means by this affirmation—how he is risen, in what sort of body, and so forth—but without the resurrection of Jesus there is not much to Christianity. It becomes merely one more probable philosophy among others. The teachings of Jesus are good, but by themselves they are no more than that. Loving one's neighbor is always good, but without the resurrection it is little more than a helpful practice. Going to church together may keep the family intact, but without the resurrection the church itself cannot hold together.

Up to this point we have been dealing with Jesus' descent—to earth in his birth, to death on the cross, to hell itself after his death. But now things have turned around. Now the one who was crucified, dead, and buried has risen again, living from among the dead! Paralleling Paul's hymn in Philippians, we now come to the point where Paul declares, "Therefore God also highly exalted him and gave him the name that is above every name, so that at the name of Jesus every knee should bend, in heaven and on earth and under the earth" (Phil. 2:9–10).

One can imagine what the Creed says about Jesus as opening with three descending steps: "was born . . . suffered . . . descended to the dead." One can then imagine the Creed closing with three steps showing his power and victory: "he ascended . . . is seated at the right hand of the Father . . . will come again to judge." Between the first three and the last three stands the resurrection.

In the literature of the time, when one wished to underline a point, one did not place it at the end of an argument, or as an opening statement, as we do today. One placed it at the very center, wrapped in concentric circles. Thus, the structure of what the Creed says about Jesus could be diagrammed as follows:

was born	will come to judge
suffered	sits on the right hand of God
descended into hell	ascended into heaven

He rose again from the dead

A similar, although simpler, structure may be found in the traditional response after the celebrant in Communion declares, "Great is the mystery of faith," and the congregation summarizes that mystery in three concentric phrases:

Christ has died,	Christ will come again.

Christ is risen,

The center of what the Creed says about Jesus is the resurrection. The resurrection is not just God's affirmation that this one who was crucified is indeed God's Son. It is not just a final miracle among many showing the power and authority of Jesus. It is the very heart of the gospel!

The Third Day

At the close of the previous chapter we imagined Jesus as a time bomb that the devil had stolen and safely locked up in his strongbox. And then, on the third day . . .

Before going much farther, one point needs clarification. I remember my perplexity when, as a young child, we spoke of the crucifixion of Jesus on Good Friday and his resurrection on Sunday morning. Counting from late Friday afternoon to early Sunday morning, I could at best come up with thirty-six hours—and thirty-six hours is not even two days! Why then did people insist that Christ had risen on the third day?

The explanation is simple. At that time people counted days, and years, much like vacation clubs and cruises count days today. If you go on an "eight-day cruise," you leave late on Monday and return early next Monday. In fact, you have had only six full days and part of two; but the company advertising the cruise counts part days as whole days. This was the customary way of counting time in the ancient world. Thus, when Paul refers to his having taught for "three years" (Acts 20:31), this may well have been as little as fourteen months—one month, a full year, and another month. According to this way of reckoning, Jesus was in the tomb three days—part of Friday, all of Saturday, and part of Sunday.

Victory and Liberation!

So it was on the third day, after the apparent victory of the forces of evil, when it would seem that injustice and death would have the last word, that he rose again. The time bomb went off. It destroyed the devil's strong box, blew his office apart, and punched a great hole on the wall holding prisoners. It is on the basis of this imagery—or rather of its equivalent in ancient times when fortunately there were no time bombs—that the most common and earliest depictions of the resurrection are not about an empty tomb; they are rather of Jesus breaking out of hell. In so doing, he not only frees himself from the power of the evil one, but he also frees others as they follow him in his escape from hell. (In some of the more dramatic paintings, we see him coming out of hell, standing on the door he has burst open, with the devil squashed under the door, and a vast multitude following him out of hell.) This is what is usually called "the harrowing of hell."

Naturally, all of this imagery is not intended to describe what actually happened on that third day, but rather to give us some understanding of why that day is so important for us and for all of creation. It also gives us a fuller picture of what Christ does for us. Since the early Middle Ages, Christians have dwelt so much on the cross and the suffering of Christ that the message of his victory has been eclipsed. Jesus Christ is not only the victim of Good Friday; he is also the victor of Easter Sunday! The one we follow and serve is not only the crucified One; he is also the risen One. He is the victor over death and evil, and it is in his victory that we too are victors.

Martin Luther put it as follows in a hymn:

> It was a strange and dreadful strife
> when life and death contended;
> the victory remained with life;
> the reign of death was ended.
> Stripped of power, no more it reigns,
> an empty tomb alone remains;
> death's sting is lost forever!
> Alleluia![1]

Luther takes the strife very seriously. It is not just a story with a happy ending. It is a dramatic struggle between the force of life and the force of death. Were we to study in more detail what Luther says about this struggle, we would find that although the victory has been won, the struggle still continues in the life of every Christian. Paul also knew of that struggle. But it is a struggle in which we do not despair, because the victory has already been won, because the love of God prevails. As Paul puts it, "In all these things we are more than conquerors through him who loved us. For I am convinced that neither death, nor life, nor angels, nor rulers, nor things present, nor things to come, nor powers, nor height, nor depth, nor anything else in all creation, will be able to separate us from the love of God in Christ Jesus our Lord" (Rom. 8:37–39).

The Third Day Is the First

The experience of that third day—the first day of the week—was so powerful that Christians began to meet every week on that day in order to celebrate it (Acts 20:7). Every Friday was a day of gloom and fasting, in remembrance of our sin and its awful price. Every Saturday—as long as most Christians were still Jewish—was a day of rest. But every Sunday was a day of feasting and celebration. In the rest of society, it was a day of work just as any other in the week. But on that day, before doing their daily chores, Christians gathered to celebrate the resurrection of their Lord. They had to meet before dawn so as not to be found remiss by their masters and supervisors, but in this too they saw a reminder of that first Easter, when "very early on the first day of the week" (Mark 16:2) the women went to the tomb and found it empty. If on Friday one fasted and humiliated oneself before the Most Holy, on Sunday one did not even kneel for prayer. Now, through the power of the resurrection, one was an adopted child of God, and therefore one approached the throne not as a supplicant but as a child approaches its parent.

They gathered to break bread. The service was long. People had no Bibles. As the number of Gentile Christians grew, they had no background knowledge of the history of what God had done or of what God demands of God's people. Therefore, the reading and exposition of Scripture took a long time. This, however, was preparation for the high point of the service, at which believers broke bread and drank wine in remembrance of Jesus. This is why Luther's hymn continues in this way:

> Then let us feast this Easter day
> on the true bread of heaven;
> the Word of grace hath purged away
> the old and wicked leaven.
> Christ alone our souls will feed;
> he is our meat and drink indeed;
> faith lives upon no other!
> Alleluia![2]

That remembrance was not only of the sacrifice of Jesus on the cross; it was also and above all a remembrance of his victory on the first day of the week. Thus, in contrast to what became common in the Middle Ages, the service of Communion was a joyful service, focusing on the resurrected One rather than only on the crucified One. In recent decades, Communion services have become more joyful, due in part to the recovery of some of the ancient practices of Christian worship and to this understanding of Communion as a remembrance of Easter. Hence the use of joyful opening words such as, "Friends, this is the joyful feast of the people of God! They will come from east and west, and from north and south, and sit at the table in the kingdom of God."[3]

The Third Day Is Also the Eighth!

According to an ancient Jewish tradition, one day the apparently end-less cycle of week after week was to come to an end. One day, after the Sabbath, instead of another first day of the week, an "eighth day" would dawn. Then would all of God's promises be fulfilled. Then the kingdom of God would come and God's *shalom* would prevail.

Christians believed—and still believe, even though we often for-get it—that this new day dawned with the resurrection of Jesus. The resurrection is not just a past event, signaling the victory of Jesus then. It is also the beginning of a new era, the dawning of the kingdom. It is, so to speak, the eighth day of creation, for which the people of God have always yearned. (This point is symbolized in the frequent octag-onal shape of baptistries and baptismal fonts.) The main difference between this and the ancient Jewish tradition is that, even though the new day has dawned and in a sense we live in it, the old days con-tinue, and we live in them too. After Sunday, when we celebrate the dawning of the new age, comes Monday, when we find ourselves liv-ing still in the old. The early Christians, while proclaiming that Jesus is Lord, still had to acknowledge that in a very real though limited sense the emperor is also lord. Those subjected under a tyrannical *paterfamilias*, while rejoicing that their true Father was God, still had to live in their own families. Today, while we proclaim the dawning of a new time of peace and justice and love, we continue living in a world of war and injustice and hatred.

This makes the affirmation of the Creed all the more important, as we seek to be sustained, so to speak, "between the times"—between the present time of strife and the already present but still future time of vic-tory. In affirming that "on the third day he rose again," we are remind-ing ourselves that the one whom we serve lives, that even though death and sin still seem to hold sway, they have been conquered.

It is this too that the church celebrates when it gathers on the first day of the week to break bread in remembrance of Christ. What we remember is not only that he suffered and died. It is not only that he triumphed in his resurrection. It is also that his victory will also be ours. It is for this reason that one of the most ancient prayers for the celebration of Communion says:

> As grain, once scattered on the hillsides
> was in broken bread made one,
> so from all lands your church be gathered
> into your kingdom by your Son.[4]

Questions for Discussion

1. Why is "Christ is risen!" such a central Christian affirmation?
2. What are the implications of Christ's resurrection for the Christian life? The church's life? The world's life?
3. In what ways are you conscious of living in the "new era" of God's kingdom, based on the resurrection of Jesus Christ?

He Ascended into Heaven, Is Seated at the Right Hand of the Father

Not Just a Footnote

Just as there is a tendency to reduce the resurrection of Jesus to a sign of God's approval, it is also true that often his ascension is reduced to a postscript to the story of Holy Week. It seems to be little more than an answer to the question, What happened to Jesus after his resurrection? Why is it that we don't see him around, as did his disciples? His ascension is almost like an epilogue in a novel, where we are told what happened to the various characters after the action ended!

But the ascension is part of the story. It is an essential part of the story. Like the resurrection, it may be interpreted in various ways. Some may think of it literally as it is told at the end of the Gospel of Luke (24:50–51) and the beginning of Acts (1:6–11). Some, insisting that heaven is not "up there," would prefer to say simply that this is Luke's way of describing the awesome experience of the disciples as Jesus left them. But, like the resurrection, we do away with it at significant loss to our faith and therefore to our daily lives.

Easter Is Not Quite Over

The ascension has several important dimensions. One of them, and perhaps the most obvious, is that in a sense Easter continues. The Lord has risen once and for all. It is important that we remember this, because in Easter season we make many references to the rebirth of all things in spring—butterflies, Easter lilies, the warmth of the sun—as images to understand the resurrection of Jesus. As images, these may be helpful, but, like all metaphorical language, they are susceptible to misinterpretation. Spring comes around every year, simply to be succeeded by summer, fall, and winter, until the next spring. We celebrate Easter every year, because we follow the cycle of the Christian year. But what we celebrate at Easter happened only once and continues to this day. The Lord who rose on that first Easter Sunday is still alive! What we celebrate at Easter is not the cyclical rebirth of nature, but the birth of a new reality, the dawn of the "eighth day," the continuous joy that our Lord lives!

Nor Is the Incarnation Over

The ascension of Jesus means that his incarnation is not over. The Jesus who rose from the dead is still as human as he ever was. He did not leave his humanity behind. The one who rose from the dead and who ascended into heaven is still one of us! His body may be different; we do not know, and it may not be important for us to know.[1] But he is still one of us. What is more, as human, he is the beginning of what we are to be. As Paul puts it, "Christ has been raised from the dead, the first fruits of those who have died" (1 Cor. 15:20). In other words, in his resurrection he is the first among many, and he continues being human, as we too will forever continue being human.

What is more, because one of us has risen from the dead and sits "on the right hand of God," we have all been given admission to the very heart of the Trinity! This may sound strange to many of us, for we have been formed in a tradition in which it is customary to emphasize God's transcendence, God's otherness, God's distance from every creature—including the human creature. There is value in this, for otherwise we would be inclined to think that there is something in us that makes us little gods, that all we have to do to be in communion with God is to fan that supposed spark of divinity in each one of us. But there is also in Christian tradition the other side of the coin. There is also the message of a God so loving that every effort is made to bring us into God's own heart. There are many who have expressed the work of Christ by declaring, for instance, that "he was made human so that humans could be made divine."[2] Commenting on this phrase, Roman Catholic theologian John L. Gresham says:

> This does not mean that human beings are absorbed in the transcendent divine essence but rather that in Christ we are invited to become members of the divine fellowship, sharing in the divine energies exchanged between Father, Son and Holy Spirit in an eternal circulation of divine life.[3]

This is not to say that we are now gods, or that we enjoy the divine attributes. We are not made omnipotent or omniscient. The Reformed tradition has rightly stressed the principle that "the finite cannot embrace the infinite." God, and God alone, is God. But what the ascension tells us is that in Christ's incarnation and ascension the infinite has embraced the finite. At the very heart of the Trinity now is this human being, Jesus. John Calvin says something similar when he declares:

> Since he entered heaven in our flesh, as if in our name, it follows, as the apostle says, that in a sense we already "sit with God in heavenly places with him" [Eph. 2:6], so that we do not await heaven with a bare hope, but in our Head already possess it.[4]

Is Seated at the Right Hand of the Father

I remember hearing these words as a child, shortly after reading *Gulliver's Travels*, and imagining Jesus sitting on the right hand of God just as a picture in my book showed a Lilliputian sitting on Gulliver's hand! Clearly, this is not what the Creed means. To sit "at" the right hand of another is to have the place of highest honor. This goes back to the time when warriors carried a shield in their left hand and an offensive weapon—a sword, lance, or mace—in their right. This made them particularly vulnerable to attack from the right, and therefore every chieftain or king placed his most trusted warrior at his right. As a result, the custom evolved of having the most honored adviser of a king sit at the right of the throne. Similar customs continue to this day, when in many cultures it is customary to seat the guest of honor at the right hand of the host or hostess. To "sit at the right hand" is therefore a sign of great favor, of shared authority.

When the Creed affirms that Jesus now "is seated at the right hand of the Father," it is affirming that he now shares in the Father's power and authority. At this point one should recall what was said in chapter 2 regarding the meaning of the word "Almighty": It refers to God's ruling power over all creation. Calvin explains:

> This is as if it were said that Christ was invested with lordship over heaven and earth, and solemnly entered into possession of the government committed to him—and that he not only entered into possession once for all, but continues in it, until he shall come down on Judgment Day.[5]

The author of Hebrews combines this point with the previous one about the presence of one of us in the very Godhead. He or she quotes the Eighth Psalm, saying about human beings, "You have crowned them with glory and honor, subjecting all things under their feet" (Heb. 2:7–8). But there is a difficulty that Hebrews points out and then solves: "We do not yet see everything in subjection to them" (2:8). The solution: "But we do see Jesus, who for a little while was made lower than the angels, now crowned with glory and honor" (2:9).

In brief, the ascension is about the victory of Jesus. It leads us back to the text from Ephesians: that Jesus "when he ascended on high he made captivity itself a captive" (Eph. 4:8). The one who in his resurrection conquered death now sits at the very throne of God, and because he is there the evil that once held us captive no longer has the power to do so. And if we once might have been inclined to fear not only the powers of evil but also God, because as sinners we could not stand God's holiness, now we know otherwise, for, as Calvin says, Jesus Christ now "fills with grace and kindness the throne that for miserable sinners would otherwise have been filled with dread."[6]

Questions for Discussion

1. In what ways is the ascension of Jesus Christ an essential part of the Christian story?
2. What does the affirmation that Jesus sits at the "right hand" of God have to do with issues of human power today?
3. Where are places in your own experience where you see the victory of Jesus affirmed?

9

And Will Come Again to Judge the Living and the Dead

A God of Justice

Christians have long had difficulties trying to decide whether ours is a God of love or a God of justice. As early as the second century, Marcion claimed that the secondary or inferior God of the Old Testament was a god of justice, while the supreme Father of Jesus Christ was a God of love. The contrast between justice and love, between a vengeful God and a loving one, led him to reject the entire history of Israel and the claim that God's revelation in Jesus Christ had antecedent or preparation in the Hebrew Scriptures. As we have seen, the church rejected this view for a number of reasons, and much of the Creed shows the church's determination to make clear that it did not hold to such views.

Even so, similar notions persist to this day. I have repeatedly heard Sunday school teachers—even ministers with seminary degrees—declare that in the Old Testament God is envisioned as legalistic and demanding, while in the New, thanks to the teachings of Jesus, God is presented as a loving Father. Even worse, there are sermons depicting the Old Testament deity as an angry God, and Jesus as the soothing, forgiving, loving one. This is simply not true. In the Old Testament, God is the faithful companion of Israel, whose many sins are repeatedly forgiven; God is the one "whose mercy endures forever," as the Psalms repeatedly declare; God is the loving husband ready to forgive his errant wife; God comforts Israel "as a mother comforts a child" (Isa. 66:13). In the New Testament, on the other

/ 66

hand, Jesus speaks of an eternal fire prepared for the devil and his angels, and of weeping and gnashing of teeth.

Perhaps what we need to do is to reconsider our concepts of both love and justice. In its most common usage both in our courts of law and in our daily conversation, "justice" has to do primarily with punishing evildoers. If a robber is condemned to jail, we say that justice was done. If a mass murderer is caught and brought to trial, people will say that justice requires the death penalty. In our daily conversation, we equate justice with someone "getting what's coming to them." Justice is when a bully gets bullied, or when a cheater gets cheated, or when a liar is discovered. In the popular mind, justice is also rewarding the good. Justice is when someone's hard work is acknowledged and celebrated, or when a good employee gets a raise, or when labor and management reach an equitable agreement.

But justice is much more than that. Justice is when everything is in its proper place. (Note the relationship between "justice" and "adjust." Adjusting things to their proper place, size, and function is a sort of justice.) Justice is when no one oppresses another, when all show mutual respect, when life and freedom and peace are affirmed. A just ruler will not only punish the evildoers and reward those who do good but will also protect the weak so that they will not be oppressed or exploited by the rest. A just ruler will not only make certain that the laws are obeyed but also that the laws themselves are just, that they do not favor the rich and the powerful so that they may become richer and more powerful. Such justice is not contrary to love but is actually a form of love.

Love, on the other hand, is not simply allowing others to do as they please. It is not saying to someone "I forgive you," as if whatever they did were unimportant and irrelevant. We must remember this, because we are often tempted to dismiss others under the subterfuge of love. "That's alright. What you did to me doesn't matter" may well be another way of saying, "That's alright. You don't matter." Love is truly concerned over the actions and the being of the beloved. A truly loving mother demands of her son that he behave, not just because this will please her but also because she knows that good behavior is good for her child. A father who allows his daughter to do as she pleases and then simply tells her it's OK is not a very good father. Love truly wishes the best for the beloved. Such love ultimately coincides with justice.

Clearly, such love and such justice are so far above our own love and our own justice that we cannot comprehend them. Hence the endless arguments among Christians, some contending that God's love demands that all be forgiven, and some insisting that God's justice must be fulfilled and that therefore there must be eternal punishment. On this score, perhaps all we can say is that our limited understanding of love does not permit us to understand how God's love can be fulfilled in conjunction with infinite justice, and that our limited understanding of justice does not allow us to understand how God's justice can be fulfilled in conjunction with infinite love.

It is to remind us of this that the Creed ends the section on Jesus by declaring that he will be the judge. Marcion could never accept that. He insisted that Yahweh is the god of judgment, and that Jesus is all-forgiving. This is a distorted view both of justice and of love, as well as of God. It solves the dilemma of our limited understanding by separating love from justice. Ours is a God of such love that it is perfect justice, and of such justice that it is perfect love.

He Will Come

Having said all of this, it is important to remember that the one who will come is the one whom we already know—the one who for our sake was born, suffered, and was crucified, dead and buried, and rose again on the third day. As we look at the throne of judgment, we shall not see there an alien, harsh judge. We shall see one who has borne our pain and suffered our infirmities. We shall see God, yes. But we shall also see one of us!

It is important for us to remember this. The judgment of God is a dreadful thing and much to be feared. But ultimately it is in that judgment that love will prevail. In judgment, God says No to our actions, to our efforts, to our very way of being, in order to say Yes to our true being and to bring it to fruition. Yet this does not make either the love or the justice any less real. As Reformed theologian Karl Barth put it, "It is evident that the Yes and No heard here are as distinct from every other Yes and No as are the heavens from the earth. It is evident that both are proclaimed unconditionally and compellingly, being limited neither by the relativity which otherwise confines their expression, nor by human incapacity to do justice to them."[1]

Ultimately, as we confront the judge of all creation, all we can do is trust, not in our good actions—which would never deserve a verdict of "not guilty"—but in the one who suffered, died, and rose again for our sake, who is also the judge. His boundless love will be joined with justice for our own good and blessing.

No one has expressed this better than John Calvin:

> Hence arises our wonderful consolation: that we perceive judgment to be in the hands of him who has already destined us to share with him the honor of judging! Far indeed is he from mounting the seat of judgment to condemn us! How could our most merciful Ruler destroy his people? How could the Head scatter its own members? . . . No mean assurance this—that we shall be brought before no other judgment seat than that of our Redeemer, to whom we must look for our salvation![2]

Questions for Discussion

1. In what ways do you understand the relationship between God's justice and God's love?
2. Many people fear the idea that Jesus will come again. Do you? Why or why not?
3. What are the comforts and challenges from realizing that our judge is also our redeemer?

No clarification possible outside it's intended. central. Talking point for sermons.

10

I Believe in the Holy Spirit

We Are Not Alone

According to the Gospel of John, when Jesus was preparing his disciples for the time when he would no longer be with them, he told them:

> I will not leave you orphaned; I am coming to you. In a little while the world will no longer see me, but you will see me; because I live, you also will live. On that day you will know that I am in my Father, and you in me, and I in you. . . . I have said these things to you while I am still with you. But the Advocate, the Holy Spirit, whom the Father will send in my name, will teach you everything, and remind you of all that I have said to you. (John 14:18–20, 25–26)

It would be a very sad state for Christians were we limited to what we have said in the Creed to this point. The last clauses on the section about Jesus end with words of absence: "He ascended into heaven, is seated at the right hand of the Father, and will come." The departure of a loved one is always a sad affair. No matter how much you believe you will see them again, you hate to see them go, to have to live without them. Imagine the feelings of the disciples, having not only heard the teaching and witnessed the deeds of Jesus but even having seen him alive after his death, now seeing their master and friend depart once more. When read with this in mind, the story of the ascension as told at the end of Luke and the beginning of Acts is poignant.

The disciples have been enjoying the company and teachings of Jesus once more. Now he takes them to a mountain, and their expectations are high. Perhaps this is the time! Perhaps it is now that he will restore the kingdom of Israel! But Jesus tells them that it is not for them to inquire when things will happen. Instead, they will receive the power of the Holy Spirit, so they may be witnesses to Jesus. And then he leaves them! The ascension, joyful and miraculous as it seems to us, would have been a very painful experience for the disciples, who stay there, gazing at the sky, until "two men in white robes" come to console them (Acts 1:6–11).

They then return to Jerusalem, and on the day of Pentecost strange things happen. For our purposes, there are a few points worth noting. The first is that the promise of Jesus not to leave his disciples orphaned is fulfilled on the day of Pentecost. Jesus had told them that the "Advocate, the Holy Spirit," would come to them, that this Advocate would be with them forever, and that thanks to this Advocate they would be in Jesus and Jesus in them—and they would even see Jesus! Because of the presence of this Advocate, the disciples would be able to live in joy even at the time of the physical absence of Jesus. Because of the presence of this same Spirit, we today can joyfully proclaim that Jesus ascended, sits at the right hand of God, and will come again. Though he is not physically with us, he is present in the Spirit.

The word that our Bibles translate as "Advocate" is *parakletos*. It is for this reason that, particularly in hymns, the Holy Spirit is called the "Paraclete." This Greek word literally means "called to be by . . . ," or "called to stand to the side of . . ." In the courts, a "paraclete" would be an advocate, a defender, but in times of sorrow a paraclete would be one mourning with the bereaved. Thus, in today's usage, a paraclete would be something like a "faithful companion," a "comforter"—as the King James Version translates the word—or a "sponsor" or "supporter." Thus, what the title ultimately means is that this other Paraclete would be the disciples' companion, much as Jesus himself—the first Paraclete—had been for several years. Left bereft of the company of Jesus, the disciples are given another companion who is so close to Jesus that by being in the Spirit the disciples will be in Jesus.

When we declare that we believe in the Holy Spirit, this believing *in* is parallel to our belief in God the Father and in Jesus. This says something both about our faith and about the Spirit. Regarding our faith, it says that it rests and lives in the Spirit. Regarding the Spirit, the same affirmation declares that the Spirit is worthy of praise and adoration, just as much as the Father and the Son.

The Spirit and Faith in Jesus

Another important point is that the presence and action of the Spirit is indissolubly linked with faith in Jesus. Paul declares that "no one can say 'Jesus is Lord' except by the Holy Spirit" (1 Cor. 12:3). Sometimes people imagine that the presence of the Holy Spirit is a higher degree of discipleship or of blessing than mere faith in Jesus. But the fact is that true faith in Jesus is always the work of the Spirit, and that therefore whenever we have such faith we may rejoice also that we have the Spirit. Likewise, Calvin affirms that "the Holy Spirit is the bond by which Christ effectually unites us to himself."[1] If we are united with Christ, this in itself is proof that we have the Holy Spirit, and if we have the Holy Spirit we also have faith in Christ.

The reason for this is that faith is not a human work. It is not something we decide on our own to have whenever we wish, as we decide to have an apple or a pear. True faith is beyond our reach and is attainable only through the grace of God, by the presence and power of the Holy Spirit.

Thus, again, believing *in* is much more than we imagine when we glibly use these words. In declaring that we believe in the Holy Spirit, we are not only affirming that we are convinced *that* there is a Holy Spirit, but also and above all that it is precisely because we are *in* the Spirit that we are able to believe—that it is out of this stance *in* the Spirit that we dare declare, "I believe in God the Father Almighty. . . . And in Jesus Christ . . ."

Likewise, just as we ourselves cannot believe in God and in Christ without the Spirit, so the ancients—Abraham, Sarah, Isaac, Rebekah —who did believe in God did so because of the Spirit. The Spirit was not a recent arrival at the time of Pentecost. The Spirit had always been there. What happened at Pentecost was that the power of the Spirit was given to the disciples so that—as Jesus had promised (Acts 1:8)—they could be witnesses.

Power for All

We must be clear how this Holy Spirit acts. Often we imagine that on that day of Pentecost it was only the twelve disciples who received the power of the Spirit. But if you read the passage in Acts 2 carefully, you will see that this is not the case. On the contrary, according to the narrative in Acts a goodly number of disciples were present, and when the tongues of fire appeared, "*all* of them were filled with the Holy Spirit, and began to speak in other languages." Were it not so, Peter's speech would make no sense, for he announces that what people are witnessing is the fulfillment of the promise of God, that "I will pour out my Spirit upon all flesh, and your sons and your daughters shall prophesy, and your young men shall see visions, and your old men shall dream dreams. Even upon my slaves, both men and women, in those days I will pour out my Spirit" (Acts 2:17–18). Peter is able to refer to this prophecy precisely because among those who have received the power of the Spirit, and are speaking in diverse tongues, are sons and daughters, young and old, menservants and maidservants.

Furthermore, the purpose for which those gathered at Pentecost received the power of the Spirit was not to have power over others but to share their power. Were it God's intention that the apostles and those like them would always hold the positions of leadership, the Spirit could have made all those present understand the language of the apostles. But as Luke tells the story, "each one heard them speaking in the native language of each" (Acts 2:6). The Spirit made it quite clear that those who spoke the Aramaic of the apostles had no advantage over Medes or Cappadocians. Once they heard the message in their own tongue, they would be free to proclaim it—just as free as the apostles themselves.

This is not the picture of the power of the Spirit we would derive from listening to many today who claim to have such power. Looking at them and their work, it would appear that they have been given the power of the Spirit so that they may be acclaimed by others, and even so that they may have authority and control over others. Sometimes—often thanks to modern mass media—people flock to them as if they had control of the power of the Spirit. But no, the power of the Spirit who worked at Pentecost is the power of the one who makes *all*—women and men, young and old, weak and powerful—hear the message in their own language and in their own circumstances.

The Holy Spirit

Why is this Spirit called "holy"? Holiness has two dimensions. First of all, it refers to that which is sacred, or has some special connection with God. Thus, Scripture proclaims that God is "holy, holy, holy," which is a Hebrew way of saying "most holy." Because of their connection with the Holy One, we speak also of the "Holy Temple" and the "Holy Land." When used in this way, to declare that we are in the presence of the Holy One is to tremble and be filled with awe.

The Spirit is holy in this sense. The Spirit is God. The Spirit is powerful. The Spirit is not a plaything, just as a live wire is not a plaything. The Spirit is not there for us to manipulate or to seek to control or to use to our advantage. We try such things at our own peril. The Spirit is holy—and this to the utmost degree.

On the other hand, this Holy One is called "Spirit." The word for "spirit," both in Greek and in Hebrew, actually means "wind." Jesus uses this dual meaning of the word in his conversation with Nicodemus: "The wind blows where it chooses, and you hear the sound of it, but you do not know where it comes from or where it goes. So it is with everyone who is born of the Spirit" (John 3:8). Here Jesus is speaking both of the power of the wind and of its freedom. The presence of the wind is known by its power, by its sound. Sometimes we experience the wind as a gentle breeze and sometimes as a frightening storm. They are both the same wind, which chooses from what direction and with what force to blow. Thus, to refer to this Holy One as Spirit is a reference both to power and to freedom. The Holy Spirit is never ours to control. The Holy Spirit is never ours to predict. The Holy Spirit repeatedly surprises us, sometimes by blowing as a gentle breeze and sometimes with thunder and hail.

Holiness has a second dimension, derived from the first. In this second sense, holiness has to do with purity and obedience. In English we have two words for what in Greek is only one: holiness and sanctity. Thus, we say that God is holy, and that Sister Helen is a saint. However, by being able to use these two words we may miss the connection between holiness and sanctity, to which we must now turn as we study the next phrases in the Creed: "the *holy* catholic church, the communion of *saints*."

Questions for Discussion

1. In what ways are you conscious of the Holy Spirit as your advocate?
2. In what ways do you experience the Holy Spirit at work in your life? In the life of the church? In the world?
3. In what ways do you experience the power and the freedom of the Holy Spirit?

The Holy Catholic Church,
the Communion of Saints

Under the Heading of the Spirit

What gave the Creed its Trinitarian structure was its early use in connection with baptism and therefore with the formula, "in the name of the Father, the Son, and the Holy Spirit." Thus, as we move to the theme of the church, in a way we are still under the heading of the Spirit—the third major heading of the Creed. Since both in Greek and in Latin there is only one word, which we translate sometimes as "holy" and sometimes as "saint," when one looks at the Creed in either of these two ancient languages in which it originally existed one sees the same word repeated: *Holy* Spirit, *holy* church, communion of the *holy*. The holiness of the last two, as all holiness, is derived from the Holy Spirit.

Furthermore, it is *in* the Spirit that we believe these clauses and all that follow. As discussed in the last chapter, all true faith comes from the Spirit and is therefore faith *in* the Spirit, which is to say that it is faith *in* this Holy One who is God.

What do we mean then by the phrase "the holy catholic church"? Leaving the word "catholic" aside for the time being, it is clear that in a sense we believe *in* the church; we are part of the church, we are believers *within* the church. This, however, is not the same sense in which we believe *in* God the Father, *in* Jesus Christ, and *in* the Spirit. Otherwise, we would fall into idolatry, placing our faith in what is not divine. The church is an essential part of the Creed because it is in it that we experience faith. In spite of all we have heard to the contrary, faith is never a purely private matter; it is always communal. It certainly is personal in the sense that each one of us must claim it for herself or himself. But it is never personal or private in the sense that it has nothing to do with the community of the faithful. John Wesley expressed this starkly when commenting on the notion of a private religion:

> Directly opposite to this is the gospel of Christ. Solitary religion is not to be found there. "Holy solitaries" is a phrase no more consistent with the gospel than holy adulterers. The gospel of Christ knows of no religion, but social; no holiness but social holiness.[1]

So the Creed affirms belief *in* the church not in the sense that the church is the object of our faith, but rather in the sense that it is within the church, in the context of the church and as members of it, that we believe.

However, this is not to be understood in the sense of "We believe the church." This is the notion of "implicit faith" that was prevalent during the Middle Ages and that the Reformation rejected. Implicit faith was tantamount to declaring, "I don't rightly know all that the church teaches, but whatever the church teaches I believe, because it is taught by the church." Against such notions, John Calvin wrote:

> Is this what believing means—to understand nothing, provided only that you submit your feeling obediently to the church? Faith rests not on ignorance, but on knowledge. . . . We do not obtain salvation either because we are prepared to embrace as true whatever the church has prescribed, or because we turn over to it the task of inquiring and knowing.[2]

In brief, we believe *in* God and in no other. We believe *in* God the Father Almighty, and *in* the Son of God, Jesus Christ, and *in* the Holy Spirit. It is thanks to the Spirit that we are in the church, which is the context of our belief.

The Holy Church

Here again we must remember the two connected but different meanings of the word "holy." In its primary, fundamental meaning, that which is holy is so close to God as to be sacred. It is only in its secondary, derivative meaning that "holy" means pure or morally perfect. Certainly, God is holy in both senses. But what do we mean when we refer to the church as holy? If we mean that it is morally spotless, this is of all the clauses in the Creed the most difficult to believe! We have all seen much—and done much—that shows that the church is not pure and unblemished.

Along these lines, think of the phrase "Holy Land." It certainly is not a land of moral perfection, where all love each other as they should. Nor is it a land of peace. Yet we call it holy. Why? Because in so designating it we remind ourselves that it is not only a land of war, terrorism, and hatred, but also the land where it has pleased God to come to us most clearly. It is the land to which Abraham and Sarah were called, where Jacob and his wives raised their children, from which Joseph went to Egypt and where his descendants eventually returned, where Samuel heard God's voice and Isaiah saw the Lord. It is the land of Peter and Mary and James and Mary Magdalene, the land where Jesus walked, the land where he shed his tears and his blood. All of this does not make it particularly pure—on the contrary, it makes its constant history of war and hatred even more tragic. But it does make it holy.

Likewise, to say that the church is holy is not to claim for it a particular level of moral purity. Yet we call it holy for the same reasons we call the land holy: This is the community of Peter and Mary and James and Mary Magdalene. This is the community in which martyrs have testified with their blood, in which missionaries have gone to distant lands for the sake of their faith, in which devout believers have devoted all their energies to the support and defense of the defenseless. This is the community in which millions upon millions—a "multitude that no one could count" (Rev. 7:9)—have found support in times of grief, and faith in times of anguish. This is the community in which my parents surrounded me with love, in which my faith grew, in which my faith has been repeatedly tested and strengthened. For all these reasons, just as that land over there is holy, this church over here and everywhere is also holy.

But above all, the church is holy because of the presence of the Holy Spirit in it. Remember that what we say in the Creed regarding the church is part of our faith in the Spirit. Ultimately, it is the Spirit, and not its moral purity, or its martyrs, or its devout people that make the church holy. To declare that the church is holy is to remind ourselves that when we are dealing with this community we are not just dealing with a group of people—perhaps very nice people, and perhaps not. We are dealing with the Most Holy Spirit of God![3]

In brief, to say that the church is holy is not to claim for it or for its members a moral purity it obviously lacks, but rather to claim for it and for its members the presence and the power of the Holy Spirit— which in turn renders our lack of moral purity even more tragic. The holiness of the church is both an affirmation about the presence of the Holy One in it and a call to it, to be more faithful to what that presence demands.

The Holy Catholic Church

The word "catholic" does not appear in R, the earliest form of the Apostles' Creed. It appears first in several creeds in the Greek-speaking branch of the church—particularly the Nicene Creed—and apparently from them made its way into the Apostles' Creed at some point toward the end of the fourth century. However, as we study early Christian literature it is clear that by the beginning of the second century this word was already becoming a special way to refer to the church at large.[4]

It is often said that this word means "universal," and that therefore it is a way of referring to the presence of the church throughout the world. This is partly true. Indeed, most early Christian writers tend to refer to the "catholic church" as the one that is present throughout the world, in contrast to the various sects, which are small and local. But the word "catholic" actually means "according to the whole," so that what makes the church catholic is not its presence everywhere, but rather the fact that people from everywhere are part of it and contribute to it. Therefore, a variety of experiences and perspectives is not contrary to the catholicity of the church; quite the contrary, it is a necessary sign of it. Using the word "catholic" in the same way, Christians would refer to the canon of Scripture—and particularly of the New Testament—as "catholic," meaning that, in contrast to various sectarians, each with their own single Gospel, the catholic canon includes a variety of Gospels. The sectarians have a single Gospel and reject all others; they have a single view and reject all others. But the "catholic" church embraces a wide variety of believers.

Thus, when in the Creed we refer to "the holy catholic church," we are not referring to a particular denomination. Quite the contrary, we are affirming the existence of the church even in the midst of our various theologies, traditions, and polities, and affirming our membership in that church.

The Communion of Saints

Of all the phrases in the Creed, this is the one whose exact meaning has been most discussed by scholars and interpreters. It appears to have been introduced into the Creed at some point in the late fourth or early fifth century.[5] Its most obvious meaning would be something like "the fellowship of believers," in which case it is little more than an explanation of "the holy catholic church." The problem is that both words in the Latin text, *communio sanctorum*, have more than one meaning.

Communio may mean fellowship, but it also means sharing. In such case, an English translation would be "the sharing of the saints," and the phrase would seem to refer to the sharing of goods described in Acts and practiced in varying degrees by the early church. At the time when this phrase was added to the Creed, such sharing had all but disappeared and was continued almost exclusively in monastic communities. Thus, the phrase could have been an attempt by monastics to call others to the level of sharing of earlier times.

Sanctorum may mean "of the saints," as most of us usually understand it, or "of holy things." In the latter case, the phrase refers to the sharing of holy things, particularly at the sacrament of Holy Communion.

Most likely, the original meaning of the phrase involved aspects of all of these. If so, when we affirm "the communion of saints" we are affirming: (1) our fellowship with believers of all times and places; (2) our readiness to share with others who are in need; (3) that our sharing includes "holy things"—in other words, that the "holy things" do not belong to some of us in particular, but to all of us as a whole.

So much for history and matters of interpretation. But what about us today? What do we mean when we recite these words in the Creed? We are certainly referring to the fellowship among believers, both present and absent. We probably are declaring that it is our sharing in "holy things" that makes us a fellowship—that it is our common faith, our common baptism, the one bread of Communion, that makes us one body. Perhaps we are even declaring ourselves ready to share with others in that fellowship.

Questions for Discussion

1. In what sense is the church holy? In what ways do you recognize the church's holiness?
2. What are the implications for affirming that the church is catholic? How should this affirmation affect the way we view other Christians?
3. What does the phrase "communion of saints" mean to you? In what ways does this affect your attitudes and life?

The Forgiveness of Sins

The Origin of the Phrase

Like "the communion of saints," the phrase "the forgiveness of sins" seems to have been added to R at some point during the fourth century. If so, it is easy to understand why. This was a time when the issue of the forgiveness of sins had become paramount. A few years earlier, after the worst of all persecutions, Emperor Constantine had put an end to persecution. Soon it became acceptable, and eventually almost mandatory, to be a Christian. Not all believers celebrated this new state of affairs. Some of the greatest preachers of all time insisted that Christianity required more than this, and called the masses to a deeper understanding of this new faith they had adopted. Others left the comforts of society, withdrawing to deserted places where they could lead a life of prayer and contemplation. While all of these continued as faithful members of the church, others declared that the church had become too lenient toward sinners—particularly those who had betrayed their faith during the recent persecutions—and therefore insisted that the only true church was theirs. While there were several such groups, the largest was the Donatists.

Donatism arose almost immediately after the end of persecution. One of the pressure points against the church during the persecution of the early fourth century had been the order to give up all copies of Scripture to be burned. To this order, Christian leaders reacted in several different ways: some refused, and were tortured and eventually killed; others gave up books they claimed were Christian Scripture when in fact they were not;

still others gave up the sacred books, arguing that it was better to save lives than to save books.[1] They were difficult times, with difficult decisions to be made, and as is usually the case, people followed different courses of action.

After the persecution ceased, many of those who had weakened under its threat now sought reconciliation with the church. After due proof of sincerity, most of them were readmitted to the church—after all, the church is supposed to be a people of love and forgiveness. But others protested. They insisted that the church is supposed to be holy and to witness to the truth of Christ. How then could it accept within its bosom those who were such clear sinners and who had denied the faith? On this basis, they rejected the rest of the church as tainted by sin and created a church of their own. Since one of their leaders was named Donatus, the rest of the church dubbed them "Donatists."

It seems to have been as a response against the rigorism of the Donatists and others like them that the phrase was added to the Creed, "the forgiveness of sins."

A Continuing Issue

The Donatist controversy was long and need not detain us here. The main point for our purposes is that it brought to the foreground the basic tension between the view of the church as the holy people of God—understanding "holiness" as moral purity—and the view of the church as the loving and forgiving people of God. This had long been a matter of some disagreement among Christians, and repeatedly had resulted in dissension and schism.[2]

The issue is still present with us today. In worship, we repeatedly confess our sinfulness, hear "words of assurance" that our sins are forgiven, and then, as "the forgiven and reconciled people of God," give each other signs of peace and love. But this only works up to a point. If someone is guilty of an egregious sin—particularly one that results in scandal—we are not sure how much to forgive, or how soon. Often such a person simply leaves the church, probably in part out of a sense of shame and in part as a result of shunning by others. Eventually, upon deciding to return to church, he or she will join a different congregation, thus avoiding further shunning and not forcing the initial congregation to decide whether to forgive or not. Such a final outcome would seem to be a denial of what we affirm in the Creed by "the forgiveness of sins."

Something similar is true at the interpersonal level. Someone hurts us in some way, and we simply refuse to forgive. We hold grudges that we simply won't let go. Or we forgive in a manner that is a surreptitious form of revenge, by telling the other that whatever he or she did is not important—which is a way of telling them they are not important. Often such attitudes affect the life of the entire community. For instance, when a proposal is made or someone takes a particular position, others take a stance, not on the basis of the value of what is being proposed or said, but rather on the basis of what that person has done to them and the grudges they still hold.

At this point the statement in the Creed helps us clarify matters. First of all, to affirm "the forgiveness of sins" is to affirm that we ourselves have been forgiven. Coming immediately after "the holy catholic church" and "the communion of saints," it means that those of us who recite these words are part of the church because we are forgiven. We declare the forgiveness of sin because without such forgiveness we would not be here, we would not be confessing this faith, we would not be part of this company. Through the action of the Holy Spirit in whom we believe, the church is the community of those who have experienced—and continue experiencing—the forgiveness of sins.

But then, to affirm the forgiveness of sin is to affirm also the forgiveness of the sins of others. There is a connection between the two. Jesus put it bluntly in his explanation of the Lord's Prayer and in a very pointed parable. Regarding the Lord's Prayer, he commented, "For if you forgive others their trespasses, your heavenly Father will also forgive you; but if you do not forgive others, neither will your Father forgive your trespasses" (Matt. 6:14–15). At first, these words seem to imply a sort of transaction: If you forgive others, God will forgive you. But the matter is much deeper. Often the reason we do not forgive others is that we ourselves are not convinced that we are forgiven. We may feel that we have done nothing that requires forgiveness. Or we may have such a sense of guilt that we can cling to our own self-worth only by considering ourselves better than those whom we refuse to forgive. In either case, we are not ready to accept

God's forgiveness. Our own nonforgiving attitude makes us incapable of being forgiven!

The parable appears in Matthew 18 and is commonly called the parable of the Unforgiving Servant. The story is about a slave who is brought before a king to render accounts and is found to owe ten thousand talents. We are so accustomed to hearing about "talents" that we do not even stop to consider what this sum means. A talent was about 6,000 denarii, which was the usual pay for a day's work. Thus, this slave owes the king the equivalent of 60,000 days' work—roughly 200 years! (At $50,000 a year, this would come to 10 million dollars.) The king forgives him his debt, and as he goes out he meets a poor fellow who owes him the approximate value of a hundred day's work. He chokes the man, demanding that the debt be paid, and when this does not succeed, he throws the man into debtors' prison. When the king hears of this he summons him and says, "You wicked slave! I forgave you all that debt because you pleaded with me. Should you not have had mercy on your fellow slave, as I had mercy on you?" (Matt. 18:32–33). Having said this, the king orders that the man be tortured until he pays all that he owes. Jesus responds, "So my heavenly Father will also do to every one of you, if you do not forgive your brother or sister from your heart" (18:35).

The point of the parable should be obvious. Before God, we are like that man whose enormous debt was forgiven. If we are in church, it is precisely because of this. We are the forgiven people of God. But now we who have been forgiven so much insist on being paid full measure for whatever others owe us. So we say, "He did not thank me after all I did for him. I shall never forgive him!" Or, "She said something about me that was not flattering, and not entirely true. I shall never forgive her!" How can we forget how much more we have been forgiven?

Then there is another point to the parable. The man who is forgiven and then tries to wring every last cent out of the poorer one is a servant of the king. When his debtor sees him coming, he sees not only a creditor but also a representative of the king. Whatever this powerful man does reflects on the king whom he serves. As he chokes the man and orders him put in prison he is saying something about himself, but he is also saying something about the king whom he serves.

The poor man, being wrung dry by the king's servant, would be led to think that the king himself is a ruthless, extortionist tyrant. Thus, by his very actions this man is speaking evil of a king who has been so kind to him.

What then about the church and its members? We claim to be servants of God and to proclaim God's love to the world. When we refuse to forgive each other, or when all that the church does is point to the shortcomings of others outside the church, how do those others see it? At best, they see us as hypocrites or as ungrateful people who claim to be forgiven sinners and yet do not really believe it or do not act as if we do. At worst, since we claim to be servants of the King, they come to the conclusion that our God is as harsh and unforgiving as we are.

Questions for Discussion

1. Why is it important for us to confess that we believe in the forgiveness of sins?
2. In what ways do our attitudes about forgiveness reflect our views of God?
3. If we experience the forgiveness of sins, what does this mean for our attitudes about the sins of others?

The Resurrection of the Body, and the Life Everlasting

Life Everlasting

The earliest forms of the Creed ended with the words now translated as "the resurrection of the body." "The life everlasting" seems to have been added not as a separate clause or a statement about a different belief, but simply as a clarification of what was meant by "the resurrection of the body." Apparently there were people who pointed out that Lazarus and others in the Bible who were brought back from the dead had died again, and thus wondered whether their own resurrection would end in a new death. In Greek and in Latin there is a single word to denote both what we now call "resuscitation" and "resurrection." Thus, the resurrection of Lazarus, which in the Gospel of John is intended as a sign of the final resurrection, led some to fear that their own final resurrection might end in another death, as in the case of Lazarus. As a twentieth-century scholar put it, this clause was added because "it is evident that many people wanted more than the assurance that they would one day rise from the dead: mere resurrection was compatible with dying again." As a result, he concludes, "the clause [life everlasting] owed its place in the creed to the desire to quieten troubled minds."[1]

The phrase itself was not new, for it appears in the New Testament over two dozen times, and in very different sorts of literature: the Synoptic Gospels, John, Acts, Romans, 1 Timothy, Titus, 1 John, and Jude. Even in those books of the New Testament where the phrase itself does not appear, the concept is clearly present. What was new in the fourth century was the addition of the phrase to the Creed. At any rate, it seems to round up the Creed nicely, concluding with an endless future.

Even so, much has been written about this phrase, in which many Christians over the years have found consolation as well as mystery. The main theme of such writings is the contrast between what we now call "life" and the real "life everlasting." As most have put it, the difference is not simply that the present life ends and the future one does not—a mere quantitative difference. The difference is also in the joy and the continuous blessedness of that future life in contrast with the constant struggle, pains, and tragedies of the present one. Probably the most famous statement of this contrast is from Augustine in the very first chapter of his *Confessions*: "[Lord,] you have made us for yourself, and our heart is restless until it rests in you."[2] Throughout many of his writings, in many but less memorable words, Augustine explains that true life is life in God and that therefore only that life which is eternal—that is, life in the presence of the Eternal—is true life.

The Resurrection of the Body, Not Just the Immortality of the Soul

It is obvious that the final resurrection of the dead was part of Christian teaching from the very beginning. In fact, the doctrine of a final resurrection existed among the Pharisees long before the advent of Christianity. The Pharisees insisted on it over against the opposition of the Sadducees. It is also evident that from a very early date there were those who had difficulties with this doctrine. This is the background of Paul's 1 Corinthians 15, which presents a very forceful argument in favor of the final resurrection, against those who would deny it.

What is being debated in that chapter, however, is not just the matter of life after death, but more concretely the resurrection of the body. The notion of life after death was quite common in the Hellenistic world into which Christianity was moving. Socrates and Plato had taught it, as did most of their disciples. They believed that the soul is immortal and that therefore when it is separated from the body the latter dies but the soul goes on living. They were also convinced that one's true self was the soul and that therefore the death and corruption of the body had little significance—or even was a positive event, a liberation of the soul from its enslavement in the body. Hence the play on words in Greek, *soma sema*—the body is a sepulcher. The Gnostics also taught the immortality of the soul, which they claimed to be a spark of divinity trapped in the body. So did Marcion, for whom "life eternal" was the liberation of the soul from the bonds of this material world created by Yahweh.

Surprising as it may seem for many Christians today, most Christian pastors and teachers saw a marked difference between the commonly held notion of the immortality of the soul and Christian teaching. That teaching was different precisely in that it included the resurrection of the body. This Christian teaching differed from the common notion of the immortality of the soul on two main scores: Christian insistence that eternal life is a gift from God, and the conviction that God's final purposes include the material as well as the spiritual.

Eternal Life as God's Gift

To speak of eternal life as what happens naturally, because the soul is immortal by its own nature, is to forget that such eternal life is always a gift of God's grace. The supposed "immortality" of the soul would mean that the soul is immortal simply because that is what it is—just as a ball is round simply because that is what it is. Socrates, for instance, discusses the matter in Plato's dialogue *Phaedo*, and comes to the conclusion "that the soul is in the very likeness of the divine, and immortal, and intelligible, and uniform, and indissoluble, and unchangeable."[3] Then he comments that those who have condemned him to death could kill his body but not his soul, because the soul is by definition life, and no one can kill life.

Early Christians found the pagan philosophers' notion of the soul and its immortality to be helpful. As they sought to respond to the mockery of their neighbors, who criticized them for believing in an afterlife, these philosophers provided a powerful rebuttal, for they too had affirmed their belief in life after death. Christians would then claim that what they taught was not so strange, for the philosophers held very similar opinions. This in turn led Christians themselves to speak more and more of the immortality of the soul, and less and less of the resurrection of the body—to the point that many came to the conclusion that what Socrates taught and what the church declares on this matter are practically the same.

Yet Christians have always insisted that there is no being that is in itself eternal, except God. All creation has come to existence because of God and continues existing because of God. Were God's sustaining power suddenly removed from creation, it would immediately vanish into nothingness. This includes the soul, which—precisely because it is a creature and not the Creator—cannot subsist without God's sustaining power.[4] It is not that we live because we have a soul, but rather that we have a soul and we live thanks to God's sustaining grace.

The Resurrection of the Body

Christians insisted on the resurrection of the body for two main reasons. The first of these was to underscore God's active role in Christian hope. What Christians hope for is not a mere continuation of what already exists; it is not the natural outcome of things as they are. If you place a ball atop a hill and let it go, it will roll downward. There is nothing unique about this. That is the way things are. The ball rolls downhill because that is what it is supposed to do, what it does out of its own nature and the forces of nature. By insisting on the resurrection of the dead, Christians made clear that what they expected was not simply the unfolding of what already exists, the working out of the nature of things. They were well aware that the resurrection of the body was not easy to accept. Their critics asked pesky questions: What happens to the bodies of those who died at sea and were eaten by fish? Will God go around collecting pieces of their bodies? What about those particles that at various times had belonged to more than one body? To whose body will they belong? Will the other bodies then have holes? To all of this—and much more along the same vein— Christians responded that the final resurrection was an act of God, an act as mighty as creation itself. The God who made all things out of nothing will have no difficulty raising the bodies of the dead, in spite of all the objections of small minds asking silly questions! The point is precisely that Christian hope rests in faith in God, and not on faith on the nature of things—not even on the nature of the soul, as did Socrates' hope.

The second reason why Christians insisted on the resurrection of the body was the need to affirm the positive value of the material. Marcion and a host of other teachers claimed that the physical world was not God's creation or part of the divine purpose but rather an obstacle standing in the way of that purpose. Salvation could have nothing to do with the material or the corporeal. Over against such teachings, the church declared its hope for the resurrection of the material body.

This theme was of such importance that the original versions of the Creed, both in Greek and in Latin, do not really say "the resurrection of *the body*," as do our modern versions. They actually say "the resurrection of *the flesh*." In most translations of the Creed into modern languages this has been changed in order to take into account what Paul says about the unknown nature of the resurrected body. Still, however, Christian hope includes the material as well as the spiritual—the body as well as the soul. Jesuit theologian Karl Rahner has put it starkly:

> We Christians are, therefore, the most sublime of materialists. We neither can nor should think of any ultimate fulness of the spirit and of reality without thinking too of matter enduring as well in a state of final perfection. It is true that we cannot picture to ourselves in the concrete how matter would have to appear in this state of final endurance and glorification, for all eternity. But we have so to love our own physicality and the worldly environment appropriate to it that we cannot reconcile ourselves to conceiving of ourselves as existing to all eternity otherwise than with the material side of our natures enduring too in a state of final perfection.[5]

This is the place at which the doctrine of the resurrection of the body has practical implications for our everyday life: "to love our own physicality and the worldly environment appropriate to it." Were we to affirm only our trust in the immortality of the soul, we could easily decide—as unfortunately many Christians have done—that all that matters is the spiritual. From that point there is only one step to the conclusion that the body is either evil or at least dispensable, and that therefore all that is important is to save souls—ours as well as those of others. Following that line of thought, there have been Christians who were convinced that in trying to force others to conversion by physical threats or even by means of torture they were doing them a favor! Even today, there are believers who question why we should feed the hungry, or seek justice for the oppressed, or care for the elderly, when our main concern should be for their eternal souls.

But we affirm "the resurrection of the body and the life everlasting." The life for which we hope is life in the body. The life we affirm is life in the body. And, as believers in this final resurrection and this life everlasting, we now live in love and respect for these bodies that are called to rise again on that joyful day!

Until then, joining countless believers throughout the world and through the ages, we dare live as those who can truly declare:

I believe in God the Father Almighty, Maker of heaven and earth.

And in Jesus Christ his only Son our Lord; who was conceived by the Holy Spirit, born of the Virgin Mary, suffered under Pontius Pilate, was crucified, dead, and buried; he descended to the dead. On the third day he rose again; he ascended into heaven, is seated at the right hand of the Father, and will come again to judge the living and the dead.

I believe in the Holy Spirit, the holy catholic church, the communion of saints, the forgiveness of sins, the resurrection of the body, and the life everlasting.

Amen! So be it!

Questions for Discussion

1. In what ways does the view of the "immortality of the soul" differ from the Creed's affirmation of the "resurrection of the body"?
2. What are implications of our confession of the "resurrection of the body" for everyday life? For our future lives?
3. Does your belief in "the life everlasting" shape your present attitudes and actions? In what ways?

Notes

Introduction

1. The story first appeared in its full form in the fourth century. Its classical summary is found in Rufinus's *Commentary on the Creed*, written early in the fifth century.
2. (Pseudo) Augustine, *Sermon* 240.
3. Hippolytus, in the third century, refers to what he considers the ancient Roman practice of asking a candidate for baptism three questions: (1) "Do you believe in God the Father almighty?" (2) Do you believe in Jesus Christ, the Son of God, who was born by the Holy Spirit from the Virgin Mary, who was crucified under Pontius Pilate, died, and rose again on the third day, living from among the dead, and ascended into the heavens, and sat at the right hand of the Father, and will come to judge the living and the dead?" (3) "Do your believe in the Holy Spirit, in the holy church, and in the resurrection of the flesh?" In the fourth century, Rufinus quotes R as follows: "I believe in God the Father almighty; and in Christ Jesus his only Son, our Lord, who was born of the Holy Spirit and the Virgin Mary, who under Pontius Pilate was crucified and buried, on the third day rose again from the dead, ascended into heaven, sits at the right of the Father, from whence he will come to judge the living and the dead, and in the Holy Spirit, the holy church, the forgiveness of sins, the resurrection of the flesh."
4. Irenaeus, writing in Gaul late in the second century, declares that the church has "received from the apostles and their disciples this faith: [She believes] in one God, the Father Almighty, Maker of heaven, and earth, and the sea, and all things that are in them; and in one Jesus Christ, the Son of God, who became incarnate for our salvation; and in the Holy Spirit, who proclaimed through the prophets the dispensations of God, and the advents, and the birth from a virgin, and the passion, and the resurrection from the dead, and the ascension

into heaven, and his [future] manifestation from heaven . . . that he should execute judgment towards all." (*Against Heresies* 1.10, in *The Ante-Nicene Fathers*, ed. Alexander Roberts and James Donaldson. 10 vols. (1867–1887; repr., Peabody, MA: Hendrickson, 1994), 1:330. Ireneaus has similar summaries in the same work, 4.2, and in *Proof of the Apostolic Preaching.* Tertullian, writing slightly later in North Africa, offers three summaries of the faith (*On the Prescription of Heretics* 36; *Against Praxeas* 2; *On the Veiling of Virgins* 1). Although none of these corresponds exactly to R, the combination of the three show that he was acquainted, if not with R, at least with a similar creed.

Chapter 1: I Believe in God the Father

1. Karl Barth, *Dogmatics in Outline* (New York: Harper Torchbooks, 1959), 16.
2. The authority of the *paterfamilias* extended to having the right to determine who among the newly born was to be a member of the family. In traditional Roman practice, when a child was born it was placed on the ground. The *paterfamilias* would then come into the room and decide whether to pick the child up or not. If he picked it up, it was considered a proper child of the household. If not, it was normally abandoned in a public place where it would either die or be picked up by someone. Christianity opposed such practices, and Christian writers during the second and third centuries used this as an argument to show the moral stature of Christianity above traditional beliefs and practices.
3. In the *Martyrdom of Sts. Perpetua and Felicitas*, a document from the early third century, we are told that Perpetua refused to obey her father, who entreated her to give up her faith. Later the Roman procurator insisted that she should do this in consideration of her father's white hair, and she still refused. Although Perpetua's father is not depicted as trying to force her to do his will, she clearly disobeyed him.

Chapter 2: Almighty, Maker of Heaven and Earth

1. For this reason, Marcion had no use for the Hebrew Scriptures, which he believed to be the word of a god, but not of the one, true, supreme God. This compelled him to make a list of a number of Christian books that he considered Christian Scripture. Since he was convinced that only Paul had understood the gospel correctly, this list included the Gospel of Luke—whom he took to be Paul's companion—and the letters of Paul. Both Luke and Paul, however, were expurgated of any reference to the Hebrew Scriptures or to creation. Marcion claimed that any such references were later interpolations

by people trying to establish connections between Christianity and Judaism—connections that did not really exist.

2. The typical way in which late medieval theologians dealt with this issue was by distinguishing between the "absolute" and the "ordered" power of God. On the basis of "absolute" power, God can do anything, including what would otherwise be evil. In this sense, whatever God does is good. But God has set a limit to this absolute power by establishing an order that even God follows. Thus, on the basis of God's "ordered" power, God always does what is good.

Chapter 3: And in Jesus Christ His Only Son Our Lord

1. At this point, one must point out that the masculine language of the traditional Trinitarian formula raises the same issues discussed earlier in the context of God as Father—now exacerbated by the reference also to God as Son. One common way of avoiding such language is to refer to God as "Creator, Redeemer, and Sustainer." Like any image, this has its advantages and disadvantages. The advantages are obvious, for this formula avoids the use of gender-specific language. The disadvantage is that it seems to base the doctrine of the Trinity on external relationships and functions—creating, sustaining, and redeeming—thus making it dependent on God's relationship with the world and saying little about the Godhead itself. A more traditional formula—using words early Christian writers used on occasion—would be "Source, Word, and Holy Spirit." This overcomes the difficulties of the "Creator, Redeemer, Sustainer" formula, but it does this at the cost of using impersonal language. In brief, all these various formulas have their shortcomings and their advantages.

2. Leonardo Boff, *Holy Trinity, Perfect Community* (Maryknoll, NY: Orbis Books, 2000), 3.

3. In the later development of doctrine, partly in order to safeguard the doctrine of the Trinity, the distinction was made between the eternal generation of the Son from the Father, so that Father, Son, and Holy Spirit are eternal, and the Son's temporal generation "by the Holy Spirit," resulting in his birth from Mary. In its early usage, however, the Creed does not seem to have concerned itself with such matters, which did not become real subjects of discussion and debate until the fourth century.

4. This martyr's name was Thelica. All that we know of his final fate is that the judge was so furious that he ordered Thelica, who had been seriously tortured, to be returned to prison until he could devise a form of death worthy of such stubbornness. *Acts of the Martyrdom of Saturninus, Dativus, and Others* 6.

5. *The Theological Declaration of Barmen* 8.11–12, in the *Book of Confessions: Study Edition* (Louisville, KY: Geneva Press, 1999), 311.

Chapter 4: Who Was Conceived by the Holy Spirit, Born of the Virgin Mary

1. See more on this in Catherine Gunsalus González and Justo Luis González, *Their Souls Did Magnify the Lord* (Atlanta: General Assembly Mission Board of the Presbyterian Church, U.S.A., 1977), 28–31.
2. Tertullian, *On the Flesh of Christ* 1, in *The Ante-Nicene Fathers*, 3:521, slightly corrected.
3. In the ninth century, Ratramnus of Corbie refuted some otherwise unknown people in Germany who claimed that Jesus was not born "through the natural door." Yet his refutation itself shows to what degree the physical virginity of Mary had become an article of faith. Thus, he declares that Jesus "came to us even while the womb was closed, just as he came to his disciples even while the doors were closed," and that "it would be senseless to think that the birth through which all things corrupt were restored would corrupt those things which were uncorrupted" (*On the Virginal Birth* 1, 2; my trans.)

Chapter 5: Suffered under Pontius Pilate, Was Crucified, Dead, and Buried

1. Ignatius, *Epistle to the Magnesians* 11 (my trans.). Similar phrases appear in his *Epistle to the Trallians* and in his *Epistle to the Smyrneans*. In the latter, he joins Herod to Pontius Pilate, declaring that Jesus "was nailed to a cross under Pontius Pilate and Herod the tetrarch" (Ign. *Smyrn.* 1).
2. Justin uses the phrase repeatedly, to the point that it appears to have been a cliche by his time. In his *First Apology* (13.3), for instance, he declares his faith in Jesus Christ, "who was crucified under Pontius Pilate, who was procurator of Judea in times of Tiberius Caesar."
3. Rufinus, *Commentary on the Creed* 18 (my trans.).
4. Ignatius, *Epistle to the Trallians* 9 (my trans.).
5. Ignatius, *Epistle to the Smyrneans* 2 (my trans.).
6. *Gospel of James* 19 (my trans.).

Chapter 6: He Descended to the Dead

1. John Wesley, "A Letter to a Roman Catholic," in *The Works of John Wesley*, ed. Jackson. 14 vols. (London: Wesleyan Conference Office, 1872), 10:82; italics are mine.
2. Tertullian, *On the Soul*, in *The Ante-Nicene Fathers*, 3:251.
3. I have written more extensively about this and other theological options in *Christian Thought Revisited: Three Types of Theology* (Maryknoll, NY: Orbis Books, 1999).

4. Irenaeus, *Against Heresies* 3.18.6, in *Ante-Nicene Fathers*, 1:447–48.
5. Ibid., 3.18.7, in *Ante-Nicene Fathers,* 1:448. I have used this translation because it is the most readily available to readers today. However,
it is important to point out that the gender-specific term "man" does
not appear in the Greek. This English translation was made at a time
when there was little or no consciousness around sexist language.

Chapter 7: On the Third Day He Rose Again

1. This translation is by Richard Massie and can be found in *The Presbyterian Hymnal* (Louisville, KY: Westminster/John Knox Press,
1990), no. 110, and in *The United Methodist Hymnal* (Nashville:
United Methodist Publishing House, 1989), no. 319.
2. Ibid.
3. *Book of Common Worship* (Louisville, KY: Westminster/John Knox
Press, 1993), 68.
4. This translation is by Fr. Bland Tucker et al. and can be found in *The
United Methodist Hymnal* (Nashville: United Methodist Publishing
House, 1989), no. 563. The original text is from the *Didache* 9.4.

Chapter 8: He Ascended into Heaven, Is Seated
at the Right Hand of the Father

1. Shortly after the Reformation, when there was sharp debate between
Lutheran and Reformed Christians on the manner of the presence of
Christ in Communion—particularly on the presence of his body—
the question of the exact nature of the resurrected body of Jesus was
also debated, for it seemed to impinge on the question of how that
body could or could not be present in Communion celebrations.
2. Athanasius, *On the Incarnation of the Word of God* 54.
3. John L. Gresham, "Three Trinitarian Spiritualities," in *Exploring
Christian Spirituality: An Ecumenical Reader*, ed. Kenneth J.
Collins (Grand Rapids: Baker Books, 2000), 287.
4. John Calvin, *Institutes of the Christian Religion* 2.16.16, ed. John T.
McNeill, trans. Ford Lewis Battles, LCC (Philadelphia: Westminster
Press, 1960), 1:524.
5. Ibid., 2.16.15.
6. Ibid., 2.16.16.

Chapter 9: And Will Come Again to Judge
the Living and the Dead

1. Karl Barth, *Church Dogmatics*, III/1 (Edinburgh: T. & T. Clark,
1958), 377.
2. Calvin, *Institutes* 2.16.18.

Chapter 10: I Believe in the Holy Spirit

1. Calvin, *Institutes* 3.1.1.

Chapter 11: The Holy Catholic Church, the Communion of Saints

1. John Wesley, preface to *Hymns and Sacred Poems* (1739), Jackson edition, 14:321.
2. Calvin, *Institutes* 3.2.2.
3. In this context, it may be helpful to point out that although the Creed says nothing to that effect, there is also within Christianity—particularly in its Eastern branches—a long and venerable tradition that speaks of "the holy world." It is not only the church, but all of creation, that is holy, because it is God's creation, because the Spirit who in the beginning "moved over the face of the waters" still moves in it. The entire created order is holy because it is in it—and only in it—that God comes to meet us.
4. The first such usage that has been preserved appears in Ignatius's *Epistle to the Smyrneans* 8.2. After that it becomes increasingly common. By the end of that second century it had become such a trademark of the church that Tertullian, writing in Latin, preferred to transliterate the Greek rather than translate it.
5. It is first quoted by Nicetas of Remisiana, who died in 414.

Chapter 12: The Forgiveness of Sins

1. These were given the name of *traditores*, meaning "those who gave to others" the Scriptures, from which we get our word "traitor." Since the same word was used for Judas, it is no surprise that animosity against the *traditores* ran high.
2. Early in the third century, there had been a disagreement between Callixtus and Hippolytus, when the former—who was bishop of Rome—declared himself ready to forgive those guilty of fornication who would confess and repent. Hippolytus had himself elected as rival bishop of Rome, and the schism continued for some time. Something similar happened, again in Rome, a few years later, when Novatian accused the bishop of that city with being too lenient toward those who had committed apostasy—that is, who had abandoned their faith—in times of persecution.

Chapter 13: The Resurrection of the Body, and Life Everlasting

1. J. N. D. Kelly, *Early Christian Creeds* (London: Longmans, Green & Co., 1950), 387.

2. Augustine, *Confessions* 1.1.
3. *The Dialogues of Plato*, trans. B. Jowett (New York: Bigflow, Brown & Co., n.d.), 3:218.
4. Medieval philosophers distinguished between "eternity" and "sempiternity." Only God is eternal, having no beginning and no end. But souls are "sempiternal," which means that they are not in themselves eternal, that their existence is constantly dependent on God, that there was a time when they did not exist, and that now they go on existing forever.
5. Karl Rahner, *Theological Investigations*, vol. 7 (London: Darton, Longman & Todd, 1971), 183.

Further Reading

Barclay, William. *The Apostles' Creed*. William Barclay Library.
   Louisville, KY: Westminster John Knox Press, 1999.
Cranfield, C. E. B. *The Apostles' Creed: A Faith to Live By*. Grand
   Rapids: Wm. B. Eerdmans Publishing Co., 1993.
Howell, James C. *The Life We Claim: The Apostles' Creed for
   Preaching, Teaching, and Worship*. Nashville: Abingdon Press,
   2005.
McGrath, Alister E. *"I Believe": Exploring the Apostles' Creed*.
   Downers Grove, IL: InterVarsity Press, 1998.
Perkins, Pheme. *What We Believe: A Biblical Catechism of the
   Apostles' Creed*. New York: Paulist Press, 1986.
Van Harn, Roger E., ed. *Exploring and Proclaiming the Apostles'
   Creed*. Grand Rapids: Wm. B. Eerdmans Publishing Co., 2004.

CPSIA information can be obtained
at www.ICGtesting.com
Printed in the USA
BVHW031312100921
616541BV00009B/53

9 780664 229337